Flint and Feather

Flint and Feather

E. Pauline Johnson

MINT EDITIONS

Flint and Feather was first published in 1900.

This edition published by Mint Editions 2021.

ISBN 9781513277424 | E-ISBN 9781513277837

Published by Mint Editions®

 MINT
EDITIONS

minteditionbooks.com

Publishing Director: Jennifer Newens
Design & Production: Rachel Lopez Metzger
Project Manager: Micaela Clark
Typesetting: Westchester Publishing Services

Contents

CANADIAN BORN

Author's Foreword

This collection of verse I have named "Flint and Feather" because of the association of ideas. Flint suggests the Red Man's weapons of war; it is the arrow tip, the heart-quality of mine own people; let it therefore apply to those poems that touch upon Indian life and love. The lyrical verse herein is as a

> *"Skyward floating feather,*
> *Sailing on summer air."*

And yet that feather may be the eagle plume that crests the head of a warrior chief; so both flint and feather bear the hall-mark of my Mohawk blood.

E.P.J.

Biographical Sketch

E. Pauline Johnson (Tekahionwake) is the youngest child of a family of four born to the late G. H. M. Johnson (Onwanonsyshon), Head Chief of the Six Nations Indians, and his wife, Emily S. Howells, a lady of pure English parentage, her birth-place being Bristol, England, but the land of her adoption was Canada.

Chief Johnson was of the renowned Mohawk tribe, and of the "Blood Royal," being a scion of one of the fifty noble families which composed the historical confederation founded by Hiawatha upwards of four hundred years ago, and known at that period as the Brotherhood of the Five Nations, but which was afterwards named the Iroquois by the early French missionaries and explorers. These Iroquois Indians have from the earliest times been famed for their loyalty to the British Crown, in defence of which they fought against both French and Colonial Revolutionists; and for which fealty they were granted the magnificent lands bordering the Grand River in the County of Brant, Ontario, and on which the tribes still live.

It was upon this Reserve, on her father's estate, "Chiefswood," that Pauline Johnson was born. And it is inevitable that the loyalty to Britain and Britain's flag which she inherited from her Red ancestors, as well as from her English mother, breathes through both her prose and poetic writings.

At an extremely early age this little Indian girl evinced an intense love of poetry; and even before she could write, composed many little childish jingles about her pet dogs and cats. She was also very fond of learning by heart anything that took her fancy, and would memorize, apparently without effort, verses that were read to her. A telling instance of this early love of poetry may be cited, when on one occasion, while she was yet a tiny child of four, a friend of her father's, who was going to a distant city, asked her what he could bring her as a present, and she replied, "Verses, please."

At twelve years of age she was writing fairly creditable poems, but was afraid to offer them for publication, lest in after years she might regret their almost inevitable crudity. So she did not publish anything until after her school days were ended.

Her education was neither extensive nor elaborate, and embraced neither High School nor College. A nursery governess for two years at home, three years at an Indian day school half a mile from her home, and two years in the central school of the City of Brantford was the extent of her educational training. But besides this she acquired a wide general knowledge, having been, through childhood and early girlhood, a great reader, especially of poetry. Before she was twelve years old she had read every line of Scott's poems, every line of Longfellow, much of Byron, Shakespeare, and such books as Addison's "Spectator," Foster's Essays and Owen Meredith.

The first periodicals to accept her poems and place them before the public were "Gems of Poetry," a small magazine published in New York, and "The Week," established by the late Professor Goldwin Smith, of Toronto, the "New York Independent," and "Toronto Saturday Night." Since then she has contributed to "The Athenaeum," "The Academy," "Black and White," "The Pall Mall Gazette," "The Daily Express," and "Canada," all of London, England; "The Review of Reviews," Paris, France; "Harper's Weekly," "New York Independent," "Outing," "The Smart Set," "Boston Transcript," "The Buffalo Express," "Detroit Free Press," "The Boys' World" (David C. Cook Publishing Co., Elgin, Illinois), "The Mothers' Magazine" (David C. Cook Publishing Co.), "The Canadian Magazine," "Toronto Saturday Night," and "The Province," Vancouver, B.C.

In 1892 the opportunity of a lifetime came to this young versifier, when Frank Yeigh, the president of the Young Liberals' Club, of Toronto, conceived the idea of having an evening of Canadian literature, at which all available Canadian authors should be guests and read from their own works.

Among the authors present on this occasion was Pauline Johnson, who contributed to the programme one of her compositions, entitled "A Cry from an Indian Wife"; and when she recited without text this much-discussed poem, which shows the Indian's side of the North-West Rebellion, she was greeted with tremendous applause from an audience which represented the best of Toronto's art, literature and culture. She was the only one on the programme who received an encore, and to this she replied with one of her favourite canoeing poems.

The following morning the entire press of Toronto asked why this young writer was not on the platform as a professional reader; while two of the dailies even contained editorials on the subject, inquiring why she had never published a volume of her poems, and insisted so strongly that the public should hear more of her, that Mr. Frank Yeigh arranged for her to give an entire evening in Association Hall within two weeks from the date of her first appearance. It was for this first recital that she wrote the poem by which she is best known, "The Song my Paddle Sings."

On this eventful occasion, owing to the natural nervousness which besets a beginner, and to the fact that she had scarcely had time to memorize her new poem, she became confused in this particular member, and forgot her lines. With true Indian impassiveness, however, she never lost her self-control, but smilingly passed over the difficulty by substituting something else; and completely won the hearts of her audience by her coolness and self-possession. The one thought uppermost in her mind, she afterwards said, was that she should not leave the platform and thereby acknowledge her defeat; and it is undoubtedly this same determination to succeed which has carried her successfully through the many years she has been before the public.

The immediate success of this entertainment caused Mr. Yeigh to undertake the management of a series of recitals for her throughout Canada, with the object of enabling her to go to England to submit her poems to a London publisher. Within two years this end was accomplished, and she spent the season of 1894 in London, and had her book of poems, "The White Wampum," accepted by John Lane, of the "Bodley Head." She carried with her letters of introduction from His Excellency the Earl of Aberdeen and Rev. Professor Clark, of Toronto University, which gave her a social and literary standing in London which left nothing to be desired.

In London she met many authors, artists and critics, who gave this young Canadian girl the right hand of fellowship; and she was received and asked to give recitals in the drawing-rooms of many diplomats, critics and members of the nobility.

Her book, "The White Wampum," was enthusiastically received by the critics and press; and was highly praised by such papers as the Edinburgh "Scotsman," "Glasgow Herald," "Manchester Guardian," "Bristol Mercury," "Yorkshire Post," "The Whitehall Review," "Pall Mall Gazette," the London "Athenaeum," the London "Academy," "Black and White," "Westminster Review," etc.

Upon her return to Canada she made her first trip to the Pacific Coast, giving recitals at all the cities and towns en route. Since then she has crossed the Rocky Mountains nineteen times, and appeared as a public entertainer at every city and town between Halifax and Vancouver.

In 1903 the George Morang Publishing Company, of Toronto, brought out her second book of poems, entitled "Canadian Born," which was so well received that the entire edition was exhausted within the year.

About this time she visited Newfoundland, taking with her letters of introduction from Sir Charles Tupper to Sir Robert Bond, the then Prime Minister of the colony. Her recital in St. John was the literary event of the season, and was given under the personal patronage of His Excellency the Governor-General and Lady McCallum, and the Admiral of the British Flagship.

After this recital in the capital Miss Johnson went to all the small seaports and to Hearts' Content, the great Atlantic Cable station, her mission being more to secure material for magazine articles on the staunch Newfoundlanders and their fishing villages than for the purpose of giving recitals.

In 1906 she returned to England, and made her first appearance in Steinway Hall, under the distinguished patronage of Lord and Lady Strathcona, to whom she carried letters of introduction from the Right Honourable Sir Wilfrid Laurier, Prime Minister of Canada. On this occasion she was accompanied by Mr. Walter McRaye, who added greatly to the Canadian interest of the programme by his inimitable renditions of Dr. Drummond's Habitant poems.

The following year she again visited London, returning by way of the United States, where she and Mr. McRaye were engaged by the American Chautauquas for a series of recitals covering eight weeks, during which time they went as far as Boulder, Colorado. Then, after one more tour of Canada, she decided to give up public work, settle down in the city of her choice, Vancouver, British Columbia, and devote herself to literature only.

Only a woman of tremendous powers of endurance could have borne up under the hardships necessarily encountered in travelling through North-Western Canada in pioneer days as Miss Johnson did; and shortly after settling down in Vancouver the exposure and hardship she had endured began to tell upon her, and her health completely broke down. For more than a year she has been an invalid; and as she was not able to attend to the business herself, a trust was formed by some of the leading citizens of her adopted city for the purpose of collecting, and publishing for her benefit, her later works. Among these is a number of beautiful Indian legends which she has been at great pains to collect; and a splendid series of boys' stories, which were exceedingly well received when they ran recently in an American boys' magazine.

During the sixteen years Miss Johnson was travelling she had many varied and interesting experiences. She has driven up the old Battleford trail before the railroad went through, and across the Boundary country in British Columbia in the romantic days of the early pioneers; and once she took an 850-mile drive up the Cariboo trail to the gold-fields. She was always an ardent canoeist, ran many strange rivers, crossed many a lonely lake, and camped in many an unfrequented place. These venturous trips she took more from her inherent love of nature and of adventure than from any necessity of her profession.

After an illness of two years' duration Miss Johnson died in Vancouver on March 7, 1913. The heroic spirit in which she endured long months of suffering is expressed in her poem entitled "And He Said 'Fight On'" which she wrote after she was informed by her physician that her illness would prove fatal.

> *Time and its ally, Dark Disarmament*
> *Have compassed me about;*
> *Have massed their armies, and on battle bent*
> *My forces put to rout,*
> *But though I fight alone, and fall, and die,*
> *Talk terms of Peace? Not I.*

It is eminently fitting that this daughter of Nature should have been laid to rest in no urban cemetery. According to her own request she was buried in Stanley Park, Vancouver's beautiful heritage of the forest primeval. A simple stone surrounded by rustic palings marks her grave and on this stone is carved the one word "Pauline." There she lies among ferns and wild flowers a short distance from Siwash Rock, the story of which she has recorded in the legends of her race. In time to come a pathway to her grave will be worn by lovers of Canadian poetry who will regard it as one of the most romantic of our literary shrines.

THE WHITE WAMPUM

(The following poems are from the author's first book, "The White Wampum," first published in 1895.)

Ojistoh

I am Ojistoh, I am she, the wife
Of him whose name breathes bravery and life
And courage to the tribe that calls him chief.
I am Ojistoh, his white star, and he
Is land, and lake, and sky—and soul to me.

Ah! but they hated him, those Huron braves,
Him who had flung their warriors into graves,
Him who had crushed them underneath his heel,
Whose arm was iron, and whose heart was steel
To all—save me, Ojistoh, chosen wife
Of my great Mohawk, white star of his life.

Ah! but they hated him, and councilled long
With subtle witchcraft how to work him wrong;
How to avenge their dead, and strike him where
His pride was highest, and his fame most fair.
Their hearts grew weak as women at his name:
They dared no war-path since my Mohawk came
With ashen bow, and flinten arrow-head
To pierce their craven bodies; but their dead
Must be avenged. Avenged? They dared not walk
In day and meet his deadly tomahawk;
They dared not face his fearless scalping knife;
So—Niyoh![1]—then they thought of me, his wife.

O! evil, evil face of them they sent
With evil Huron speech: "Would I consent
To take of wealth? be queen of all their tribe?
Have wampum ermine?" Back I flung the bribe
Into their teeth, and said, "While I have life
Know this—Ojistoh is the Mohawk's wife."

---

1. God, in the Mohawk language.

Wah! how we struggled! But their arms were strong.
They flung me on their pony's back, with thong
Round ankle, wrist, and shoulder. Then upleapt
The one I hated most: his eye he swept
Over my misery, and sneering said,
"Thus, fair Ojistoh, we avenge our dead."

And we two rode, rode as a sea wind-chased,
I, bound with buckskin to his hated waist,
He, sneering, laughing, jeering, while he lashed
The horse to foam, as on and on we dashed.
Plunging through creek and river, bush and trail,
On, on we galloped like a northern gale.
At last, his distant Huron fires aflame
We saw, and nearer, nearer still we came.

I, bound behind him in the captive's place,
Scarcely could see the outline of his face.
I smiled, and laid my cheek against his back:
"Loose thou my hands," I said. "This pace let slack.
Forget we now that thou and I are foes.
I like thee well, and wish to clasp thee close;
I like the courage of thine eye and brow;
I like thee better than my Mohawk now."

He cut the cords; we ceased our maddened haste
I wound my arms about his tawny waist;
My hand crept up the buckskin of his belt;
His knife hilt in my burning palm I felt;
One hand caressed his cheek, the other drew
The weapon softly—"I love you, love you,"
I whispered, "love you as my life."
And—buried in his back his scalping knife.

Ha! how I rode, rode as a sea wind-chased,
Mad with sudden freedom, mad with haste,
Back to my Mohawk and my home. I lashed
That horse to foam, as on and on I dashed.
Plunging thro' creek and river, bush and trail,

On, on I galloped like a northern gale.
And then my distant Mohawk's fires aflame
I saw, as nearer, nearer still I came,
My hands all wet, stained with a life's red dye,
But pure my soul, pure as those stars on high—
"My Mohawk's pure white star, Ojistoh, still am I."

As Red Men Die

Captive! Is there a hell to him like this?
A taunt more galling than the Huron's hiss?
He—proud and scornful, he—who laughed at law,
He—scion of the deadly Iroquois,
He—the bloodthirsty, he—the Mohawk chief,
He—who despises pain and sneers at grief,
Here in the hated Huron's vicious clutch,
That even captive he disdains to touch!

Captive! But *never* conquered; Mohawk brave
Stoops not to be to *any* man a slave;
Least, to the puny tribe his soul abhors,
The tribe whose wigwams sprinkle Simcoe's shores.
With scowling brow he stands and courage high,
Watching with haughty and defiant eye
His captors, as they council o'er his fate,
Or strive his boldness to intimidate.
Then fling they unto him the choice;

                              "Wilt thou
Walk o'er the bed of fire that waits thee now—
Walk with uncovered feet upon the coals,
Until thou reach the ghostly Land of Souls,
And, with thy Mohawk death-song please our ear?
Or wilt thou with the women rest thee here?"
His eyes flash like an eagle's, and his hands
Clench at the insult. Like a god he stands.
"Prepare the fire!" he scornfully demands.

He knoweth not that this same jeering band
Will bite the dust—will lick the Mohawk's hand;
Will kneel and cower at the Mohawk's feet;
Will shrink when Mohawk war drums wildly beat.

His death will be avenged with hideous hate
By Iroquois, swift to annihilate

His vile detested captors, that now flaunt
Their war clubs in his face with sneer and taunt,
Not thinking, soon that reeking, red, and raw,
Their scalps will deck the belts of Iroquois.

The path of coals outstretches, white with heat,
A forest fir's length—ready for his feet.
Unflinching as a rock he steps along
The burning mass, and sings his wild war song;
Sings, as he sang when once he used to roam
Throughout the forests of his southern home,
Where, down the Genesee, the water roars,
Where gentle Mohawk purls between its shores,
Songs, that of exploit and of prowess tell;
Songs of the Iroquois invincible.

Up the long trail of fire he boasting goes,
Dancing a war dance to defy his foes.
His flesh is scorched, his muscles burn and shrink,
But still he dances to death's awful brink.

The eagle plume that crests his haughty head
Will *never* droop until his heart be dead.
Slower and slower yet his footstep swings,
Wilder and wilder still his death-song rings,
Fiercer and fiercer thro' the forest bounds
His voice that leaps to Happier Hunting Grounds.
One savage yell—

           Then loyal to his race,
He bends to death—but *never* to disgrace.

The Pilot of the Plains

"False," they said, "thy Pale-face lover, from the land of waking morn;
Rise and wed thy Redskin wooer, nobler warrior ne'er was born;
Cease thy watching, cease thy dreaming,
    Show the white thine Indian scorn."

Thus they taunted her, declaring, "He remembers naught of thee:
Likely some white maid he wooeth, far beyond the inland sea."
But she answered ever kindly,
    "He will come again to me,"

Till the dusk of Indian summer crept athwart the western skies;
But a deeper dusk was burning in her dark and dreaming eyes,
As she scanned the rolling prairie,
    Where the foothills fall, and rise.

Till the autumn came and vanished, till the season of the rains,
Till the western world lay fettered in midwinter's crystal chains,
Still she listened for his coming,
    Still she watched the distant plains.

Then a night with nor'land tempest, nor'land snows a-swirling fast,
Out upon the pathless prairie came the Pale-face through the blast,
Calling, calling, "Yakonwita,
    I am coming, love, at last."

Hovered night above, about him, dark its wings and cold and dread;
Never unto trail or tepee were his straying footsteps led;
Till benumbed, he sank, and pillowed
    On the drifting snows his head,

Saying, "O! my Yakonwita call me, call me, be my guide
To the lodge beyond the prairie—for I vowed ere winter died
I would come again, beloved;
    I would claim my Indian bride."

"Yakonwita, Yakonwita!" Oh, the dreariness that strains
Through the voice that calling, quivers, till a whisper but remains,
"Yakonwita, Yakonwita,
    I am lost upon the plains."

But the Silent Spirit hushed him, lulled him as he cried anew,
"Save me, save me! O! beloved, I am Pale but I am true.
Yakonwita, Yakonwita,
    I am dying, love, for you."

Leagues afar, across the prairie, she had risen from her bed,
Roused her kinsmen from their slumber: "He has come to-night," she
    said.
"I can hear him calling, calling;
    But his voice is as the dead.

"Listen!" and they sate all silent, while the tempest louder grew,
And a spirit-voice called faintly, "I am dying, love, for you."
Then they wailed, "O! Yakonwita.
    He was Pale, but he was true."

Wrapped she then her ermine round her, stepped without the tepee
    door,
Saying, "I must follow, follow, though he call for evermore,
Yakonwita, Yakonwita;"
    And they never saw her more.

Late at night, say Indian hunters, when the starlight clouds or wanes,
Far away they see a maiden, misty as the autumn rains,
Guiding with her lamp of moonlight
    Hunters lost upon the plains.

The Cattle Thief

They were coming across the prairie, they were
    galloping hard and fast;
For the eyes of those desperate riders had sighted
    their man at last—
Sighted him off to Eastward, where the Cree
    encampment lay,
Where the cotton woods fringed the river, miles and
    miles away.
Mistake him? Never! Mistake him? the famous
    Eagle Chief!
That terror to all the settlers, that desperate Cattle
    Thief—
That monstrous, fearless Indian, who lorded it over
    the plain,
Who thieved and raided, and scouted, who rode like
    a hurricane!
But they've tracked him across the prairie; they've
    followed him hard and fast;
For those desperate English settlers have sighted
    their man at last.

Up they wheeled to the tepees, all their British
    blood aflame,
Bent on bullets and bloodshed, bent on bringing
    down their game;
But they searched in vain for the Cattle Thief: that
    lion had left his lair,
And they cursed like a troop of demons—for the
    women alone were there.
"The sneaking Indian coward," they hissed; "he
    hides while yet he can;
He'll come in the night for cattle, but he's scared
    to face a *man*."
"Never!" and up from the cotton woods rang the
    voice of Eagle Chief;

And right out into the open stepped, unarmed, the
    Cattle Thief.
Was that the game they had coveted? Scarce fifty
    years had rolled
Over that fleshless, hungry frame, starved to the
    bone and old;
Over that wrinkled, tawny skin, unfed by the
    warmth of blood.
Over those hungry, hollow eyes that glared for the
    sight of food.

He turned, like a hunted lion: "I know not fear,"
    said he;
And the words outleapt from his shrunken lips in
    the language of the Cree.
"I'll fight you, white-skins, one by one, till I
    kill you *all*," he said;
But the threat was scarcely uttered, ere a dozen
    balls of lead
Whizzed through the air about him like a shower
    of metal rain,
And the gaunt old Indian Cattle Thief dropped
    dead on the open plain.
And that band of cursing settlers gave one
    triumphant yell,
And rushed like a pack of demons on the body that
    writhed and fell.
"Cut the fiend up into inches, throw his carcass
    on the plain;
Let the wolves eat the cursed Indian, he'd have
    treated us the same."
A dozen hands responded, a dozen knives gleamed
    high,
But the first stroke was arrested by a woman's
    strange, wild cry.
And out into the open, with a courage past
    belief,
She dashed, and spread her blanket o'er the corpse
    of the Cattle Thief;

And the words outleapt from her shrunken lips in
    the language of the Cree,
"If you mean to touch that body, you must cut
    your way through *me*."
And that band of cursing settlers dropped
    backward one by one,
For they knew that an Indian woman roused, was
    a woman to let alone.
And then she raved in a frenzy that they scarcely
    understood,
Raved of the wrongs she had suffered since her
    earliest babyhood:
"Stand back, stand back, you white-skins, touch
    that dead man to your shame;
You have stolen my father's spirit, but his body I
    only claim.
You have killed him, but you shall not dare to
    touch him now he's dead.
You have cursed, and called him a Cattle Thief,
    though you robbed him first of bread—
Robbed him and robbed my people—look there, at
    that shrunken face,
Starved with a hollow hunger, we owe to you and
    your race.
What have you left to us of land, what have you
    left of game,
What have you brought but evil, and curses since
    you came?
How have you paid us for our game? how paid us
    for our land?
By a *book*, to save our souls from the sins *you*
    brought in your other hand.
Go back with your new religion, we never have
    understood
Your robbing an Indian's *body*, and mocking his
    soul with food.
Go back with your new religion, and find—if find
    you can—

The *honest* man you have ever made from out a
    starving man.

You say your cattle are not ours, your meat is not
    our meat;

When *you* pay for the land you live in, *we'll* pay
    for the meat we eat.

Give back our land and our country, give back our
    herds of game;

Give back the furs and the forests that were ours
    before you came;

Give back the peace and the plenty. Then come
    with your new belief,

And blame, if you dare, the hunger that *drove* him to
    be a thief."

A Cry From an Indian Wife

My forest brave, my Red-skin love, farewell;
We may not meet to-morrow; who can tell
What mighty ills befall our little band,
Or what you'll suffer from the white man's hand?
Here is your knife! I thought 'twas sheathed for aye.
No roaming bison calls for it to-day;
No hide of prairie cattle will it maim;
The plains are bare, it seeks a nobler game:
'Twill drink the life-blood of a soldier host.
Go; rise and strike, no matter what the cost.
Yet stay. Revolt not at the Union Jack,
Nor raise Thy hand against this stripling pack
Of white-faced warriors, marching West to quell
Our fallen tribe that rises to rebel.
They all are young and beautiful and good;
Curse to the war that drinks their harmless blood.
Curse to the fate that brought them from the East
To be our chiefs—to make our nation least
That breathes the air of this vast continent.
Still their new rule and council is well meant.
They but forget we Indians owned the land
From ocean unto ocean; that they stand
Upon a soil that centuries agone
Was our sole kingdom and our right alone.
They never think how they would feel to-day,
If some great nation came from far away,
Wresting their country from their hapless braves,
Giving what they gave us—but wars and graves.
Then go and strike for liberty and life,
And bring back honour to your Indian wife.
Your wife? Ah, what of that, who cares for me?
Who pities my poor love and agony?
What white-robed priest prays for your safety here,
As prayer is said for every volunteer
That swells the ranks that Canada sends out?
Who prays for vict'ry for the Indian scout?

E. PAULINE JOHNSON

Who prays for our poor nation lying low?
None—therefore take your tomahawk and go.
My heart may break and burn into its core,
But I am strong to bid you go to war.
Yet stay, my heart is not the only one
That grieves the loss of husband and of son;
Think of the mothers o'er the inland seas;
Think of the pale-faced maiden on her knees;
One pleads her God to guard some sweet-faced child
That marches on toward the North-West wild.
The other prays to shield her love from harm,
To strengthen his young, proud uplifted arm.
Ah, how her white face quivers thus to think,
Your tomahawk his life's best blood will drink.
She never thinks of my wild aching breast,
Nor prays for your dark face and eagle crest
Endangered by a thousand rifle balls,
My heart the target if my warrior falls.
O! coward self I hesitate no more;
Go forth, and win the glories of the war.
Go forth, nor bend to greed of white men's hands,
By right, by birth we Indians own these lands,
Though starved, crushed, plundered, lies our nation low. . .
Perhaps the white man's God has willed it so.

Dawendine

There's a spirit on the river, there's a ghost upon the shore,
They are chanting, they are singing through the starlight evermore,
As they steal amid the silence,
    And the shadows of the shore.

You can hear them when the Northern candles light the Northern sky,
Those pale, uncertain candle flames, that shiver, dart and die,
Those dead men's icy finger tips,
    Athwart the Northern sky.

You can hear the ringing war-cry of a long-forgotten brave
Echo through the midnight forest, echo o'er the midnight wave,
And the Northern lanterns tremble
    At the war-cry of that brave.

And you hear a voice responding, but in soft and tender song;
It is Dawendine's spirit singing, singing all night long;
And the whisper of the night wind
    Bears afar her Spirit song.

And the wailing pine trees murmur with their voice attuned to hers,
Murmur when they 'rouse from slumber as the night wind through
    them stirs;
And you listen to their legend,
    And their voices blend with hers.

There was feud and there was bloodshed near the river by the hill;
And Dawendine listened, while her very heart stood still:
Would her kinsman or her lover
    Be the victim by the hill?

Who would be the great unconquered? who come boasting how he
    dealt
Death? and show his rival's scalplock fresh and bleeding at his belt.
Who would say, "O Dawendine!
    Look upon the death I dealt?"

And she listens, listens, listens—till a war-cry rends the night,
Cry of her victorious lover, monarch he of all the height;
And his triumph wakes the horrors,
    Kills the silence of the night.

Heart of her! it throbs so madly, then lies freezing in her breast,
For the icy hand of death has chilled the brother she loved best;
And her lover dealt the death-blow;
    And her heart dies in her breast.

And she hears her mother saying, "Take thy belt of wampum white;
Go unto yon evil savage while he glories on the height;
Sing and sue for peace between us:
    At his feet lay wampum white.

"Lest thy kinsmen all may perish, all thy brothers and thy sire
Fall before his mighty hatred as the forest falls to fire;
Take thy wampum pale and peaceful,
    Save thy brothers, save thy sire."

And the girl arises softly, softly slips toward the shore;
Loves she well the murdered brother, loves his hated foeman more,
Loves, and longs to give the wampum;
    And she meets him on the shore.

"Peace," she sings, "O mighty victor, Peace! I bring thee wampum white.
Sheathe thy knife whose blade has tasted my young kinsman's blood
        to-night
Ere it drink to slake its thirsting,
    I have brought thee wampum white."

Answers he, "O Dawendine! I will let thy kinsmen be,
I accept thy belt of wampum; but my hate demands for me
That they give their fairest treasure,
    Ere I let thy kinsmen be.

"Dawendine, for thy singing, for thy suing, war shall cease;
For thy name, which speaks of dawning, *Thou* shalt be the dawn of
        peace;

For thine eyes whose purple shadows tell of dawn,
    My hate shall cease.

"Dawendine, Child of Dawning, hateful are thy kin to me;
Red my fingers with their heart blood, but my heart is red for thee:
Dawendine, Child of Dawning,
    Wilt thou fail or follow me?"

And her kinsmen still are waiting her returning from the night,
Waiting, waiting for her coming with her belt of wampum white;
But forgetting all, she follows,
    Where he leads through day or night.

There's a spirit on the river, there's a ghost upon the shore,
And they sing of love and loving through the starlight evermore,
As they steal amid the silence,
    And the shadows of the shore.

E. PAULINE JOHNSON

WOLVERINE

"Yes, sir, it's quite a story, though you won't believe it's true,
But such things happened often when I lived beyond the Soo."
And the trapper tilted back his chair and filled his pipe anew.

"I ain't thought of it neither fer this many 'n many a day,
Although it used to haunt me in the years that's slid away,
The years I spent a-trappin' for the good old Hudson's Bay.

"Wild? You bet, 'twas wild then, an' few an' far between
The squatters' shacks, for whites was scarce as furs when things is
    green,
An' only reds an' 'Hudson's' men was all the folk I seen.

"No. Them old Indyans ain't so bad, not if you treat 'em square.
Why, I lived in amongst 'em all the winters I was there,
An' I never lost a copper, an' I never lost a hair.

"But I'd have lost my life the time that you've heard tell about;
I don't think I'd be settin' here, but dead beyond a doubt,
If that there Indyan 'Wolverine' jest hadn't helped me out.

"'Twas freshet time, 'way back, as long as sixty-six or eight,
An' I was comin' to the Post that year a kind of late,
For beaver had been plentiful, and trappin' had been great.

"One day I had been settin' traps along a bit of wood,
An' night was catchin' up to me jest faster 'an it should,
When all at once I heard a sound that curdled up my blood.

"It was the howl of famished wolves—I didn't stop to think
But jest lit out across for home as quick as you could wink,
But when I reached the river's edge I brought up at the brink.

"That mornin' I had crossed the stream straight on a sheet of ice
An' now, God help me! There it was, churned up an' cracked to dice,
The flood went boiling past—I stood like one shut in a vice.

"No way ahead, no path aback, trapped like a rat ashore,
 With naught but death to follow, and with naught but death afore;
 The howl of hungry wolves aback—ahead, the torrent's roar.

"An' then—a voice, an Indyan voice, that called out clear and clean,
 'Take Indyan's horse, I run like deer, wolf can't catch Wolverine.'
 I says, 'Thank Heaven.' There stood the chief I'd nicknamed Wolverine.

"I leapt on that there horse, an' then jest like a coward fled,
 An' left that Indyan standin' there alone, as good as dead,
 With the wolves a-howlin' at his back, the swollen stream ahead.

"I don't know how them Indyans dodge from death the way they do,
 You won't believe it, sir, but what I'm tellin' you is true,
 But that there chap was 'round next day as sound as me or you.

"He came to get his horse, but not a cent he'd take from me.
 Yes, sir, you're right, the Indyans now ain't like they used to be;
 We've got 'em sharpened up a bit an' *now* they'll take a fee.

"No, sir, you're wrong, they ain't no 'dogs.' I'm not through tellin' yet;
 You'll take that name right back again, or else jest out you get!
 You'll take that name right back when you hear all this yarn, I bet.

"It happened that same autumn, when some Whites was comin' in,
 I heard the old Red River carts a-kickin' up a din,
 So I went over to their camp to see an English skin.

"They said, 'They'd had an awful scare from Injuns,' an' they swore
 That savages had come around the very night before
 A-brandishing their tomahawks an' painted up for war.

"But when their plucky Englishmen had put a bit of lead
 Right through the heart of one of them, an' rolled him over, dead,
 The other cowards said that they had come on peace instead.

"'That they (the Whites) had lost some stores, from off their little pack,
 An' that the Red they peppered dead had followed up their track,
 Because he'd found the packages an' came *to give them back*.'

E. PAULINE JOHNSON

"'Oh!' they said, 'they were quite sorry, but it wasn't like as if
They had killed a decent Whiteman by mistake or in a tiff,
It was only some old Injun dog that lay there stark an' stiff.'

"I said, 'You are the meanest dogs that ever yet I seen,'
Then I rolled the body over as it lay out on the green;
I peered into the face—My God! 'twas poor old Wolverine."

The Vagabonds

What saw you in your flight to-day,
Crows, awinging your homeward way?

Went you far in carrion quest,
Crows, that worry the sunless west?

Thieves and villains, you shameless things!
Black your record as black your wings.

Tell me, birds of the inky hue,
Plunderous rogues—to-day have you

Seen with mischievous, prying eyes
Lands where earlier suns arise?

Saw you a lazy beck between
Trees that shadow its breast in green,

Teased by obstinate stones that lie
Crossing the current tauntingly?

Fields abloom on the farther side
With purpling clover lying wide—

Saw you there as you circled by,
Vale-environed a cottage lie,

Girt about with emerald bands,
Nestling down in its meadow lands?

Saw you this on your thieving raids?
Speak—you rascally renegades!

Thieved you also away from me
Olden scenes that I long to see?

If, O! crows, you have flown since morn
Over the place where I was born,

Forget will I, how black you were
Since dawn, in feather and character;

Absolve will I, your vagrant band
Ere you enter your slumberland.

The Song My Paddle Sings

West wind, blow from your prairie nest,
Blow from the mountains, blow from the west.
The sail is idle, the sailor too;
O! wind of the west, we wait for you.
Blow, blow!
I have wooed you so,
But never a favour you bestow.
You rock your cradle the hills between,
But scorn to notice my white lateen.

I stow the sail, unship the mast:
I wooed you long but my wooing's past;
My paddle will lull you into rest.
O! drowsy wind of the drowsy west,
Sleep, sleep,
By your mountain steep,
Or down where the prairie grasses sweep!
Now fold in slumber your laggard wings,
For soft is the song my paddle sings.

August is laughing across the sky,
Laughing while paddle, canoe and I,
Drift, drift,
Where the hills uplift
On either side of the current swift.

The river rolls in its rocky bed;
My paddle is plying its way ahead;
Dip, dip,
While the waters flip
In foam as over their breast we slip.

And oh, the river runs swifter now;
The eddies circle about my bow.
Swirl, swirl!

How the ripples curl
In many a dangerous pool awhirl!

And forward far the rapids roar,
Fretting their margin for evermore.
Dash, dash,
With a mighty crash,
They seethe, and boil, and bound, and splash.

Be strong, O paddle! be brave, canoe!
The reckless waves you must plunge into.
Reel, reel.
On your trembling keel,
But never a fear my craft will feel.

We've raced the rapid, we're far ahead!
The river slips through its silent bed.
Sway, sway,
As the bubbles spray
And fall in tinkling tunes away.

And up on the hills against the sky,
A fir tree rocking its lullaby,
Swings, swings,
Its emerald wings,
Swelling the song that my paddle sings.

The Camper

Night 'neath the northern skies, lone, black, and grim:
Naught but the starlight lies 'twixt heaven, and him.

Of man no need has he, of God, no prayer;
He and his Deity are brothers there.

Above his bivouac the firs fling down
Through branches gaunt and black, their needles brown.

Afar some mountain streams, rockbound and fleet,
Sing themselves through his dreams in cadence sweet,

The pine trees whispering, the heron's cry,
The plover's passing wing, his lullaby.

And blinking overhead the white stars keep
Watch o'er his hemlock bed—his sinless sleep.

At Husking Time

At husking time the tassel fades
To brown above the yellow blades,
    Whose rustling sheath enswathes the corn
    That bursts its chrysalis in scorn
Longer to lie in prison shades.

Among the merry lads and maids
The creaking ox-cart slowly wades
Twixt stalks and stubble, sacked and torn
At husking time.

The prying pilot crow persuades
The flock to join in thieving raids;
The sly racoon with craft inborn
His portion steals; from plenty's horn
His pouch the saucy chipmunk lades
At husking time.

WORKWORN

Across the street, an humble woman lives;
To her 'tis little fortune ever gives;
Denied the wines of life, it puzzles me
To know how she can laugh so cheerily.
This morn I listened to her softly sing,
And, marvelling what this effect could bring
I looked: 'twas but the presence of a child
Who passed her gate, and looking in, had smiled.
But self-encrusted, I had failed to see
The child had also looked and laughed to me.
My lowly neighbour thought the smile God-sent,
And singing, through the toilsome hours she went.
O! weary singer, I have learned the wrong
Of taking gifts, and giving naught of song;
I thought my blessings scant, my mercies few,
Till I contrasted them with yours, and you;
To-day I counted much, yet wished it more—
While but a child's bright smile was all your store,

If I had thought of all the stormy days,
That fill some lives that tread less favoured ways,
How little sunshine through their shadows gleamed,
My own dull life had much the brighter seemed;
If I had thought of all the eyes that weep
Through desolation, and still smiling keep,
That see so little pleasure, so much woe,
My own had laughed more often long ago;
If I had thought how leaden was the weight
Adversity lays at my kinsman's gate,
Of that great cross my next door neighbour bears,
My thanks had been more frequent in my prayers;
If I had watched the woman o'er the way,
Workworn and old, who labours day by day,
Who has no rest, no joy to call her own,
My tasks, my heart, had much the lighter grown.

EASTER

April 1, 1888

Lent gathers up her cloak of sombre shading
    In her reluctant hands.
Her beauty heightens, fairest in its fading,
    As pensively she stands
Awaiting Easter's benediction falling,
    Like silver stars at night,
Before she can obey the summons calling
    Her to her upward flight,
Awaiting Easter's wings that she must borrow
    Ere she can hope to fly—
Those glorious wings that we shall see to-morrow
    Against the far, blue sky.
Has not the purple of her vesture's lining
    Brought calm and rest to all?
Has her dark robe had naught of golden shining
    Been naught but pleasure's pall?
Who knows? Perhaps when to the world returning
    In youth's light joyousness,
We'll wear some rarer jewels we found burning
    In Lent's black-bordered dress.
So hand in hand with fitful March she lingers
    To beg the crowning grace
Of lifting with her pure and holy fingers
    The veil from April's face.
Sweet, rosy April—laughing, sighing, waiting
    Until the gateway swings,
And she and Lent can kiss between the grating
    Of Easter's tissue wings.
Too brief the bliss—the parting comes with sorrow.
    Good-bye dear Lent, good-bye!
We'll watch your fading wings outlined to-morrow
    Against the far blue sky.

ERIE WATERS

A dash of yellow sand,
Wind-scattered and sun-tanned;
Some waves that curl and cream along the margin of the strand;
And, creeping close to these
Long shores that lounge at ease,
Old Erie rocks and ripples to a fresh sou'-western breeze.

A sky of blue and grey;
Some stormy clouds that play
At scurrying up with ragged edge, then laughing blow away,
Just leaving in their trail
Some snatches of a gale;
To whistling summer winds we lift a single daring sail.

O! wind so sweet and swift,
O! danger-freighted gift
Bestowed on Erie with her waves that foam and fall and lift,
We laugh in your wild face,
And break into a race
With flying clouds and tossing gulls that weave and interlace.

The Flight of the Crows

The autumn afternoon is dying o'er
    The quiet western valley where I lie
Beneath the maples on the river shore,
    Where tinted leaves, blue waters and fair sky
    Environ all; and far above some birds are flying by

To seek their evening haven in the breast
    And calm embrace of silence, while they sing
Te Deums to the night, invoking rest
    For busy chirping voice and tired wing—
    And in the hush of sleeping trees their sleeping cradles swing.

In forest arms the night will soonest creep,
    Where sombre pines a lullaby intone,
Where Nature's children curl themselves to sleep,
    And all is still at last, save where alone
    A band of black, belated crows arrive from lands unknown.

Strange sojourn has been theirs since waking day,
    Strange sights and cities in their wanderings blend
With fields of yellow maize, and leagues away
    With rivers where their sweeping waters wend
    Past velvet banks to rocky shores, in canyons bold to end.

O'er what vast lakes that stretch superbly dead,
    Till lashed to life by storm-clouds, have they flown?
In what wild lands, in laggard flight have led
    Their aerial career unseen, unknown,
    'Till now with twilight come their cries in lonely monotone?

The flapping of their pinions in the air
    Dies in the hush of distance, while they light
Within the fir tops, weirdly black and bare,
    That stand with giant strength and peerless height,
    To shelter fairy, bird and beast throughout the closing night.

Strange black and princely pirates of the skies,
    Would that your wind-tossed travels I could know!
Would that my soul could see, and, seeing, rise
    To unrestricted life where ebb and flow
    Of Nature's pulse would constitute a wider life below!

Could I but live just here in Freedom's arms,
    A kingly life without a sovereign's care!
Vain dreams! Day hides with closing wings her charms,
    And all is cradled in repose, save where
    Yon band of black, belated crows still frets the evening air.

Moonset

Idles the night wind through the dreaming firs,
That waking murmur low,
As some lost melody returning stirs
The love of long ago;
And through the far, cool distance, zephyr fanned.
The moon is sinking into shadow-land.

The troubled night-bird, calling plaintively,
Wanders on restless wing;
The cedars, chanting vespers to the sea,
Await its answering,
That comes in wash of waves along the strand,
The while the moon slips into shadow-land.

O! soft responsive voices of the night
I join your minstrelsy,
And call across the fading silver light
As something calls to me;
I may not all your meaning understand,
But I have touched your soul in shadow-land.

MARSHLANDS

A thin wet sky, that yellows at the rim,
And meets with sun-lost lip the marsh's brim.

The pools low lying, dank with moss and mould,
Glint through their mildews like large cups of gold.

Among the wild rice in the still lagoon,
In monotone the lizard shrills his tune.

The wild goose, homing, seeks a sheltering,
Where rushes grow, and oozing lichens cling.

Late cranes with heavy wing, and lazy flight,
Sail up the silence with the nearing night.

And like a spirit, swathed in some soft veil,
Steals twilight and its shadows o'er the swale.

Hushed lie the sedges, and the vapours creep,
Thick, grey and humid, while the marshes sleep.

JOE

An Etching

A meadow brown; across the yonder edge
A zigzag fence is ambling; here a wedge
Of underbush has cleft its course in twain,
Till where beyond it staggers up again;
The long, grey rails stretch in a broken line
Their ragged length of rough, split forest pine,
And in their zigzag tottering have reeled
In drunken efforts to enclose the field,
Which carries on its breast, September born,
A patch of rustling, yellow, Indian corn.
Beyond its shrivelled tassels, perched upon
The topmost rail, sits Joe, the settler's son,
A little semi-savage boy of nine.
Now dozing in the warmth of Nature's wine,
His face the sun has tampered with, and wrought,
By heated kisses, mischief, and has brought
Some vagrant freckles, while from here and there
A few wild locks of vagabond brown hair
Escape the old straw hat the sun looks through,
And blinks to meet his Irish eyes of blue.
Barefooted, innocent of coat or vest,
His grey checked shirt unbuttoned at his chest,
Both hardy hands within their usual nest—
His breeches pockets—so, he waits to rest
His little fingers, somewhat tired and worn,
That all day long were husking Indian corn.
His drowsy lids snap at some trivial sound,
With lazy yawns he slips towards the ground,
Then with an idle whistle lifts his load
And shambles home along the country road
That stretches on, fringed out with stumps and weeds,
And finally unto the backwoods leads,
Where forests wait with giant trunk and bough
The axe of pioneer, the settler's plough.

SHADOW RIVER

Muskoka

A stream of tender gladness,
Of filmy sun, and opal tinted skies;
Of warm midsummer air that lightly lies
In mystic rings,
Where softly swings
The music of a thousand wings
That almost tones to sadness.

Midway 'twixt earth and heaven,
A bubble in the pearly air, I seem
To float upon the sapphire floor, a dream
Of clouds of snow,
Above, below,
Drift with my drifting, dim and slow,
As twilight drifts to even.

The little fern-leaf, bending
Upon the brink, its green reflection greets,
And kisses soft the shadow that it meets
With touch so fine,
The border line
The keenest vision can't define;
So perfect is the blending.

The far, fir trees that cover
The brownish hills with needles green and gold,
The arching elms o'erhead, vinegrown and old,
Repictured are
Beneath me far,
Where not a ripple moves to mar
Shades underneath, or over.

Mine is the undertone;
The beauty, strength, and power of the land

Will never stir or bend at my command;
But all the shade
Is marred or made,
If I but dip my paddle blade;
And it is mine alone.

O! pathless world of seeming!
O! pathless life of mine whose deep ideal
Is more my own than ever was the real.
For others Fame
And Love's red flame,
And yellow gold: I only claim
The shadows and the dreaming.

Rainfall

From out the west, where darkling storm-clouds float,
The 'waking wind pipes soft its rising note.

From out the west, o'erhung with fringes grey,
The wind preludes with sighs its roundelay,

Then blowing, singing, piping, laughing loud,
It scurries on before the grey storm-cloud;

Across the hollow and along the hill
It whips and whirls among the maples, till

With boughs upbent, and green of leaves blown wide,
The silver shines upon their underside.

A gusty freshening of humid air,
With showers laden, and with fragrance rare;

And now a little sprinkle, with a dash
Of great cool drops that fall with sudden splash;

Then over field and hollow, grass and grain,
The loud, crisp whiteness of the nearing rain.

Under Canvas

In Muskoka

Lichens of green and grey on every side;
And green and grey the rocks beneath our feet;
Above our heads the canvas stretching wide;
And over all, enchantment rare and sweet.

Fair Rosseau slumbers in an atmosphere
That kisses her to passionless soft dreams.
O! joy of living we have found thee here,
And life lacks nothing, so complete it seems.

The velvet air, stirred by some elfin wings,
Comes swinging up the waters and then stills
Its voice so low that floating by it sings
Like distant harps among the distant hills.

Across the lake the rugged islands lie,
Fir-crowned and grim; and further in the view
Some shadows seeming swung 'twixt cloud and sky,
Are countless shores, a symphony of blue.

Some northern sorceress, when day is done,
Hovers where cliffs uplift their gaunt grey steeps,
Bewitching to vermilion Rosseau's sun,
That in a liquid mass of rubies sleeps.

The scent of burning leaves, the camp-fire's blaze,
The great logs cracking in the brilliant flame,
The groups grotesque, on which the firelight plays,
Are pictures which Muskoka twilights frame.

And Night, star-crested, wanders up the mere
With opiates for idleness to quaff,
And while she ministers, far off I hear
The owl's uncanny cry, the wild loon's laugh.

The Birds' Lullaby

I

Sing to us, cedars; the twilight is creeping
    With shadowy garments, the wilderness through;
All day we have carolled, and now would be sleeping,
    So echo the anthems we warbled to you;
        While we swing, swing,
        And your branches sing,
    And we drowse to your dreamy whispering.

II

Sing to us, cedars; the night-wind is sighing,
    Is wooing, is pleading, to hear you reply;
And here in your arms we are restfully lying,
    And longing to dream to your soft lullaby;
        While we swing, swing,
        And your branches sing,
    And we drowse to your dreamy whispering.

III

Sing to us, cedars; your voice is so lowly,
    Your breathing so fragrant, your branches so strong;
Our little nest-cradles are swaying so slowly,
    While zephyrs are breathing their slumberous song.
        And we swing, swing,
        While your branches sing,
    And we drowse to your dreamy whispering.

OVERLOOKED

Sleep, with her tender balm, her touch so kind,
     Has passed me by;
Afar I see her vesture, velvet-lined,
     Float silently;
O! Sleep, my tired eyes had need of thee!
Is thy sweet kiss not meant to-night for me?

Peace, with the blessings that I longed for so,
     Has passed me by;
Where'er she folds her holy wings I know
     All tempests die;
O! Peace, my tired soul had need of thee!
Is thy sweet kiss denied alone to me?

Love, with her heated touches, passion-stirred,
     Has passed me by.
I called, "O stay thy flight," but all unheard
     My lonely cry:
O! Love, my tired heart had need of thee!
Is thy sweet kiss withheld alone from me?

Sleep, sister-twin of Peace, my waking eyes
     So weary grow!
O! Love, thou wanderer from Paradise,
     Dost thou not know
How oft my lonely heart has cried to thee?
But Thou, and Sleep, and Peace, come not to me.

Fasting

'Tis morning now, yet silently I stand,
Uplift the curtain with a weary hand,
Look out while darkness overspreads the way,
        And long for day.

Calm peace is frighted with my mood to-night,
Nor visits my dull chamber with her light,
To guide my senses into her sweet rest
        And leave me blest.

Long hours since the city rocked and sung
Itself to slumber: only the stars swung
Aloft their torches in the midnight skies
        With watchful eyes.

No sound awakes; I, even, breathe no sigh,
Nor hear a single footstep passing by;
Yet I am not alone, for now I feel
        A presence steal

Within my chamber walls; I turn to see
The sweetest guest that courts humanity;
With subtle, slow enchantment draws she near,
        And Sleep is here.

What care I for the olive branch of Peace?
Kind Sleep will bring a thrice-distilled release,
Nepenthes, that alone her mystic hand
        Can understand.

And so she bends, this welcome sorceress,
To crown my fasting with her light caress.
Ah, sure my pain will vanish at the bliss
        Of her warm kiss.

But still my duty lies in self-denial;
I must refuse sweet Sleep, although the trial
Will reawaken all my depth of pain.
                So once again

I lift the curtain with a weary hand,
With more than sorrow, silently I stand,
Look out while darkness overspreads the way,
                And long for day.

"Go, Sleep," I say, "before the darkness die,
To one who needs you even more than I,
For I can bear my part alone, but he
                Has need of thee.

"His poor tired eyes in vain have sought relief,
His heart more tired still, with all its grief;
His pain is deep, while mine is vague and dim,
                Go thou to him.

"When thou hast fanned him with thy drowsy wings,
And laid thy lips upon the pulsing strings
That in his soul with fret and fever burn,
                To me return."

She goes. The air within the quiet street
Reverberates to the passing of her feet;
I watch her take her passage through the gloom
                To your dear home.

Beloved, would you knew how sweet to me
Is this denial, and how fervently
I pray that Sleep may lift you to her breast,
                And give you rest—

A privilege that she alone can claim.
Would that my heart could comfort you the same,
But in the censer Sleep is swinging high,
                All sorrows die.

She comes not back, yet all my miseries
Wane at the thought of your calm sleeping eyes—
Wane, as I hear the early matin bell
       The dawn foretell.

And so, dear heart, still silently I stand,
Uplift the curtain with a weary hand,
The long, long night has bitter been and lone,
       But now 'tis gone.

Dawn lights her candles in the East once more,
And darkness flees her chariot before;
The Lenten morning breaks with holy ray,
       And it is day!

CHRISTMASTIDE

I may not go to-night to Bethlehem,
Nor follow star-directed ways, nor tread
The paths wherein the shepherds walked, that led
To Christ, and peace, and God's good will to men.

I may not hear the Herald Angel's song
Peal through the Oriental skies, nor see
The wonder of that Heavenly company
Announce the King the world had waited long.

The manger throne I may not kneel before,
Or see how man to God is reconciled,
Through pure St. Mary's purer, holier child;
The human Christ these eyes may not adore.

I may not carry frankincense and myrrh
With adoration to the Holy One;
Nor gold have I to give the Perfect Son,
To be with those wise kings a worshipper.

Not mine the joy that Heaven sent to them,
For ages since Time swung and locked his gates,
But I may kneel without—the star still waits
To guide me on to holy Bethlehem.

CLOSE BY

So near at hand (our eyes o'erlooked its nearness
In search of distant things)
A dear dream lay—perchance to grow in dearness
Had we but felt its wings
Astir. The air our very breathing fanned
It was so near at hand.

Once, many days ago, we almost held it,
The love we so desired;
But our shut eyes saw not, and fate dispelled it
Before our pulses fired
To flame, and errant fortune bade us stand
Hand almost touching hand.

I sometimes think had we two been discerning,
The by-path hid away
From others' eyes had then revealed its turning
To us, nor led astray
Our footsteps, guiding us into love's land
That lay so near at hand.

So near at hand, dear heart, could we have known it!
Throughout those dreamy hours,
Had either loved, or loving had we shown it,
Response had sure been ours;
We did not know that heart could heart command,
And love so near at hand!

What then availed the red wine's subtle glisten?
We passed it blindly by,
And now what profit that we wait and listen
Each for the other's heart beat? Ah! the cry
Of love o'erlooked still lingers, you and I
Sought heaven afar, we did not understand
'Twas—once so near at hand.

The Idlers

The sun's red pulses beat,
Full prodigal of heat,
Full lavish of its lustre unrepressed;
But we have drifted far
From where his kisses are,
And in this landward-lying shade we let our paddles rest.

The river, deep and still,
The maple-mantled hill,
The little yellow beach whereon we lie,
The puffs of heated breeze,
All sweetly whisper—These
Are days that only come in a Canadian July.

So, silently we two
Lounge in our still canoe,
Nor fate, nor fortune matters to us now:
So long as we alone
May call this dream our own,
The breeze may die, the sail may droop, we care not when or how.

Against the thwart, near by,
Inactively you lie,
And all too near my arm your temple bends.
Your indolently crude,
Abandoned attitude,
Is one of ease and art, in which a perfect languor blends.

Your costume, loose and light,
Leaves unconcealed your might
Of muscle, half suspected, half defined;
And falling well aside,
Your vesture opens wide,
Above your splendid sunburnt throat that pulses unconfined.

With easy unreserve,
Across the gunwale's curve,
Your arm superb is lying, brown and bare;
Your hand just touches mine
With import firm and fine,
(I kiss the very wind that blows about your tumbled hair).

Ah! Dear, I am unwise
In echoing your eyes
Whene'er they leave their far-off gaze, and turn
To melt and blur my sight;
For every other light
Is servile to your cloud-grey eyes, wherein cloud shadows burn.

But once the silence breaks,
But once your ardour wakes
To words that humanize this lotus-land;
So perfect and complete
Those burning words and sweet,
So perfect is the single kiss your lips lay on my hand.

The paddles lie disused,
The fitful breeze abused,
Has dropped to slumber, with no after-blow;
And hearts will pay the cost,
For you and I have lost
More than the homeward blowing wind that died an hour ago.

At Sunset

To-night the west o'er-brims with warmest dyes;
Its chalice overflows
With pools of purple colouring the skies,
Aflood with gold and rose;
And some hot soul seems throbbing close to mine,
As sinks the sun within that world of wine.

I seem to hear a bar of music float
And swoon into the west;
My ear can scarcely catch the whispered note,
But something in my breast
Blends with that strain, till both accord in one,
As cloud and colour blend at set of sun.

And twilight comes with grey and restful eyes,
As ashes follow flame.
But O! I heard a voice from those rich skies
Call tenderly my name;
It was as if some priestly fingers stole
In benedictions o'er my lonely soul.

I know not why, but all my being longed
And leapt at that sweet call;
My heart outreached its arms, all passion thronged
And beat against Fate's wall,
Crying in utter homesickness to be
Near to a heart that loves and leans to me.

Penseroso

Soulless is all humanity to me
To-night. My keenest longing is to be
Alone, alone with God's grey earth that seems
Pulse of my pulse and consort of my dreams.

To-night my soul desires no fellowship,
Or fellow-being; crave I but to slip
Thro' space on space, till flesh no more can bind,
And I may quit for aye my fellow kind.

Let me but feel athwart my cheek the lash
Of whipping wind, but hear the torrent dash
Adown the mountain steep, 'twere more my choice
Than touch of human hand, than human voice.

Let me but wander on the shore night-stilled,
Drinking its darkness till my soul is filled;
The breathing of the salt sea on my hair,
My outstretched hands but grasping empty air.

Let me but feel the pulse of Nature's soul
Athrob on mine, let seas and thunders roll
O'er night and me; sands whirl; winds, waters beat;
For God's grey earth has no cheap counterfeit.

RE-VOYAGE

What of the days when we two dreamed together?
    Days marvellously fair,
As lightsome as a skyward floating feather
    Sailing on summer air—
Summer, summer, that came drifting through
Fate's hand to me, to you.

What of the days, my dear? I sometimes wonder
    If you too wish this sky
Could be the blue we sailed so softly under,
    In that sun-kissed July;
Sailed in the warm and yellow afternoon,
With hearts in touch and tune.

Have you no longing to re-live the dreaming,
    Adrift in my canoe?
To watch my paddle blade all wet and gleaming
    Cleaving the waters through?
To lie wind-blown and wave-caressed, until
Your restless pulse grows still?

Do you not long to listen to the purling
    Of foam athwart the keel?
To hear the nearing rapids softly swirling
    Among their stones, to feel
The boat's unsteady tremor as it braves
The wild and snarling waves?

What need of question, what of your replying?
    Oh! well I know that you
Would toss the world away to be but lying
    Again in my canoe,
In listless indolence entranced and lost,
Wave-rocked, and passion tossed.

Ah me! my paddle failed me in the steering
　　Across love's shoreless seas;
All reckless, I had ne'er a thought of fearing
　　Such dreary days as these,
When through the self-same rapids we dash by,
My lone canoe and I.

E. PAULINE JOHNSON

Brier

Good Friday

Because, dear Christ, your tender, wounded arm
 Bends back the brier that edges life's long way,
That no hurt comes to heart, to soul no harm,
 I do not feel the thorns so much to-day.

Because I never knew your care to tire,
 Your hand to weary guiding me aright,
Because you walk before and crush the brier,
 It does not pierce my feet so much to-night.

Because so often you have hearkened to
 My selfish prayers, I ask but one thing now,
That these harsh hands of mine add not unto
 The crown of thorns upon your bleeding brow.

WAVE-WON

To-night I hunger so,
Beloved one, to know
If you recall and crave again the dream
That haunted our canoe,
And wove its witchcraft through
Our hearts as 'neath the northern night we sailed the northern stream.

Ah! dear, if only we
As yesternight could be
Afloat within that light and lonely shell,
To drift in silence till
Heart-hushed, and lulled and still
The moonlight through the melting air flung forth its fatal spell.

The dusky summer night,
The path of gold and white
The moon had cast across the river's breast,
The shores in shadows clad,
The far-away, half-sad
Sweet singing of the whip-poor-will, all soothed our souls to rest.

You trusted I could feel
My arm as strong as steel,
So still your upturned face, so calm your breath,
While circling eddies curled,
While laughing rapids whirled
From boulder unto boulder, till they dashed themselves to death.

Your splendid eyes aflame
Put heaven's stars to shame,
Your god-like head so near my lap was laid—
My hand is burning where
It touched your wind-blown hair,
As sweeping to the rapids verge, I changed my paddle blade.

The boat obeyed my hand,
Till wearied with its grand
Wild anger, all the river lay aswoon,
And as my paddle dipped,
Thro' pools of pearl it slipped
And swept beneath a shore of shade, beneath a velvet moon.

To-night, again dream you
Our spirit-winged canoe
Is listening to the rapids purling past?
Where, in delirium reeled
Our maddened hearts that kneeled
To idolize the perfect world, to taste of love at last.

The Happy Hunting Grounds

Into the rose gold westland, its yellow prairies roll,
World of the bison's freedom, home of the Indian's soul.
Roll out, O seas! in sunlight bathed,
Your plains wind-tossed, and grass enswathed.

Farther than vision ranges, farther than eagles fly,
Stretches the land of beauty, arches the perfect sky,
Hemm'd through the purple mists afar
By peaks that gleam like star on star.

Fringing the prairie billows, fretting horizon's line,
Darkly green are slumb'ring wildernesses of pine,
Sleeping until the zephyrs throng
To kiss their silence into song.

Whispers freighted with odour swinging into the air,
Russet needles as censers swing to an altar, where
The angels' songs are less divine
Than duo sung twixt breeze and pine.

Laughing into the forest, dimples a mountain stream,
Pure as the airs above it, soft as a summer dream,
O! Lethean spring thou'rt only found
Within this ideal hunting ground.

Surely the great Hereafter cannot be more than this,
Surely we'll see that country after Time's farewell kiss.
Who would his lovely faith condole?
Who envies not the Red-skin's soul,

Sailing into the cloud land, sailing into the sun,
Into the crimson portals ajar when life is done?
O! dear dead race, my spirit too
Would fain sail westward unto you.

In the Shadows

I am sailing to the leeward,
Where the current runs to seaward
    Soft and slow,
Where the sleeping river grasses
Brush my paddle as it passes
    To and fro.

On the shore the heat is shaking
All the golden sands awaking
    In the cove;
And the quaint sand-piper, winging
O'er the shallows, ceases singing
    When I move.

On the water's idle pillow
Sleeps the overhanging willow,
    Green and cool;
Where the rushes lift their burnished
Oval heads from out the tarnished
    Emerald pool.

Where the very silence slumbers,
Water lilies grow in numbers,
    Pure and pale;
All the morning they have rested,
Amber crowned, and pearly crested,
    Fair and frail.

Here, impossible romances,
Indefinable sweet fancies,
    Cluster round;
But they do not mar the sweetness
Of this still September fleetness
    With a sound.

I can scarce discern the meeting
Of the shore and stream retreating,
    So remote;
For the laggard river, dozing,
Only wakes from its reposing
    Where I float.

Where the river mists are rising,
All the foliage baptizing
    With their spray;
There the sun gleams far and faintly,
With a shadow soft and saintly,
    In its ray.

And the perfume of some burning
Far-off brushwood, ever turning
    To exhale
All its smoky fragrance dying,
In the arms of evening lying,
    Where I sail.

My canoe is growing lazy,
In the atmosphere so hazy,
    While I dream;
Half in slumber I am guiding,
Eastward indistinctly gliding
    Down the stream.

E. PAULINE JOHNSON

NOCTURNE

Night of Mid-June, in heavy vapours dying,
Like priestly hands thy holy touch is lying
Upon the world's wide brow;
God-like and grand all nature is commanding
The "peace that passes human understanding";
I, also, feel it now.

What matters it to-night, if one life treasure
I covet, is not mine! Am I to measure
The gifts of Heaven's decree
By my desires? O! life for ever longing
For some far gift, where many gifts are thronging,
God wills, it may not be.

Am I to learn that longing, lifted higher,
Perhaps will catch the gleam of sacred fire
That shows my cross is gold?
That underneath this cross—however lowly,
A jewel rests, white, beautiful and holy,
Whose worth can not be told.

Like to a scene I watched one day in wonder:—
A city, great and powerful, lay under
A sky of grey and gold;
The sun outbreaking in his farewell hour,
Was scattering afar a yellow shower
Of light, that aureoled

With brief hot touch, so marvellous and shining,
A hundred steeples on the sky out-lining,
Like network threads of fire;
Above them all, with halo far outspreading,
I saw a golden cross in glory heading
A consecrated spire:

I only saw its gleaming form uplifting,
Against the clouds of grey to seaward drifting,
And yet I surely know
Beneath the seen, a great unseen is resting,
For while the cross that pinnacle is cresting,
An Altar lies below.

*   *   *   *   *

Night of Mid-June, so slumberous and tender,
Night of Mid-June, transcendent in thy splendour
Thy silent wings enfold
And hush my longing, as at thy desire
All colour fades from round that far-off spire,
Except its cross of gold.

My English Letter

When each white moon, her lantern idly swinging,
    Comes out to join the star night-watching band,
Across the grey-green sea, a ship is bringing
    For me a letter, from the Motherland.

Naught would I care to live in quaint old Britain,
    These wilder shores are dearer far to me,
Yet when I read the words that hand has written,
    The parent sod more precious seems to be.

Within that folded note I catch the savour
    Of climes that make the Motherland so fair,
Although I never knew the blessed favour
    That surely lies in breathing English air.

Imagination's brush before me fleeing,
    Paints English pictures, though my longing eyes
Have never known the blessedness of seeing
    The blue that lines the arch of English skies.

And yet my letter brings the scenes I covet,
    Framed in the salt sea winds, aye more in dreams
I almost see the face that bent above it,
    I almost touch that hand, so near it seems.

Near, for the very grey-green sea that dashes
    'Round these Canadian coasts, rolls out once more
To Eastward, and the same Atlantic splashes
    Her wild white spray on England's distant shore.

Near, for the same young moon so idly swinging
    Her threadlike crescent bends the selfsame smile
On that old land from whence a ship is bringing
    My message from the transatlantic Isle.

Thus loves my heart that far old country better,
    Because of those dear words that always come,
With love enfolded in each English letter
    That drifts into my sun-kissed Western home.

CANADIAN BORN

(The following poems are from the author's second book, "Canadian Born," first published in 1903.)

Canadian Born

We first saw light in Canada, the land beloved of God;
We are the pulse of Canada, its marrow and its blood:
And we, the men of Canada, can face the world and brag
That we were born in Canada beneath the British flag.

Few of us have the blood of kings, few are of courtly birth,
But few are vagabonds or rogues of doubtful name and worth;
And all have one credential that entitles us to brag—
That we were born in Canada beneath the British flag.

We've yet to make our money, we've yet to make our fame,
But we have gold and glory in our clean colonial name;
And every man's a millionaire if only he can brag
That he was born in Canada beneath the British flag.

No title and no coronet is half so proudly worn
As that which we inherited as men Canadian born.
We count no man so noble as the one who makes the brag
That he was born in Canada beneath the British flag.

The Dutch may have their Holland, the Spaniard have his Spain,
The Yankee to the south of us must south of us remain;
For not a man dare lift a hand against the men who brag
That they were born in Canada beneath the British flag.

Where Leaps the Ste. Marie

I

What dream you in the night-time
　　When you whisper to the moon?
What say you in the morning?
　　What do you sing at noon?
When I hear your voice uplifting,
Like a breeze through branches sifting,
And your ripples softly drifting
　　To the August airs a-tune.

II

Lend me your happy laughter,
　　Ste. Marie, as you leap;
Your peace that follows after
　　Where through the isles you creep.
Give to me your splendid dashing,
Give your sparkles and your splashing,
Your uphurling waves down crashing,
　　Then, your aftermath of sleep.

Harvest Time

Pillowed and hushed on the silent plain,
Wrapped in her mantle of golden grain,

Wearied of pleasuring weeks away,
Summer is lying asleep to-day,—

Where winds come sweet from the wild-rose briers
And the smoke of the far-off prairie fires;

Yellow her hair as the goldenrod,
And brown her cheeks as the prairie sod;

Purple her eyes as the mists that dream
At the edge of some laggard sun-drowned stream;

But over their depths the lashes sweep,
For Summer is lying to-day asleep.

The north wind kisses her rosy mouth,
His rival frowns in the far-off south,

And comes caressing her sunburnt cheek,
And Summer awakes for one short week,—

Awakes and gathers her wealth of grain,
Then sleeps and dreams for a year again.

LADY LORGNETTE

I

Lady Lorgnette, of the lifted lash,
    The curling lip and the dainty nose,
The shell-like ear where the jewels flash,
    The arching brow and the languid pose,
The rare old lace and the subtle scents,
    The slender foot and the fingers frail,—
I may act till the world grows wild and tense,
    But never a flush on your features pale.
The footlights glimmer between us two,—
    You in the box and I on the boards,—
I am only an actor, Madame, to you,
    A mimic king 'mid his mimic lords,
For you are the belle of the smartest set,
           Lady Lorgnette.

II

Little Babette, with your eyes of jet,
    Your midnight hair and your piquant chin,
Your lips whose odours of violet
    Drive men to madness and saints to sin,—
I see you over the footlights' glare
    Down in the pit 'mid the common mob,—
Your throat is burning, and brown, and bare,
    You lean, and listen, and pulse, and throb;
The viols are dreaming between us two,
    And my gilded crown is no make-believe,
I am more than an actor, dear, to you,
    For you called me your king but yester eve,
And your heart is my golden coronet,
           Little Babette.

          E. PAULINE JOHNSON

LOW TIDE AT ST. ANDREWS

(New Brunswick)

The long red flats stretch open to the sky,
Breathing their moisture on the August air.
The seaweeds cling with flesh-like fingers where
The rocks give shelter that the sands deny;
And wrapped in all her summer harmonies
St. Andrews sleeps beside her sleeping seas.

The far-off shores swim blue and indistinct,
Like half-lost memories of some old dream.
The listless waves that catch each sunny gleam
Are idling up the waterways land-linked,
And, yellowing along the harbour's breast,
The light is leaping shoreward from the west.

And naked-footed children, tripping down,
Light with young laughter, daily come at eve
To gather dulse and sea clams and then heave
Their loads, returning laden to the town,
Leaving a strange grey silence when they go,—
The silence of the sands when tides are low.

Beyond the Blue

I

Speak of you, sir? You bet he did. Ben Fields was far too sound
To go back on a fellow just because he weren't around.
Why, sir, he thought a lot of you, and only three months back
Says he, "The Squire will some time come a-snuffing out our track
And give us the surprise." And so I got to thinking then
That any day you might drop down on Rove, and me, and Ben.
And now you've come for nothing, for the lad has left us two,
And six long weeks ago, sir, he went up beyond the blue.

Who's Rove? Oh, he's the collie, and the only thing on earth
That I will ever love again. Why, Squire, that dog is worth
More than you ever handled, and that's quite a piece, I know.
Ah, there the beggar is!—come here, you scalawag! and show
Your broken leg all bandaged up. Yes, sir, it's pretty sore;
I did it,—curse me,—and I think I feel the pain far more
Than him, for somehow I just feel as if I'd been untrue
To what my brother said before he went beyond the blue.

You see, the day before he died he says to me, "Say, Ned,
Be sure you take good care of poor old Rover when I'm dead,
And maybe he will cheer your lonesome hours up a bit,
And when he takes to you just see that you're deserving it."
Well, Squire, it wasn't any use. I tried, but couldn't get
The friendship of that collie, for I needed it, you bet.
I might as well have tried to get the moon to help me through,
For Rover's heart had gone with Ben, 'way up beyond the blue.

He never seemed to take to me nor follow me about,
For all I coaxed and petted, for my heart was starving out
For want of some companionship,—I thought, if only he
Would lick my hand or come and put his head aside my knee,
Perhaps his touch would scatter something of the gloom away.
But all alone I had to live until there came a day

When, tired of the battle, as you'd have tired too,
I wished to heaven I'd gone with Ben, 'way up beyond the blue.

* * * *

One morning I took out Ben's gun, and thought I'd hunt all day,
And started through the clearing for the bush that forward lay,
When something made me look around—I scarce believed my mind—
But, sure enough, the dog was following right close behind.
A feeling first of joy, and than a sharper, greater one
Of anger came, at knowing 'twas not me, but Ben's old gun,
That Rove was after,—well, sir, I just don't mind telling you,
But I forgot that moment Ben was up beyond the blue.

Perhaps it was but jealousy—perhaps it was despair,
But I just struck him with the gun and broke the bone right there;
And then—my very throat seemed choked, for he began to whine
With pain—God knows how tenderly I took that dog of mine
Up in my arms, and tore my old red necktie into bands
To bind the broken leg, while there he lay and licked my hands;
And though I cursed my soul, it was the brightest day I knew,
Or even cared to live, since Ben went up beyond the blue.

I tell you, Squire, I nursed him just as gently as could be,
And now I'm all the world to him, and he's the world to me.
Look, sir, at that big, noble soul, right in his faithful eyes,
The square, forgiving honesty that deep down in them lies.
Eh, Squire? What's that you say? *He's got no soul?* I tell you, then,
He's grander and he's better than the mass of what's called men;
And I guess he stands a better chance than many of us do
Of seeing Ben some day again, 'way up beyond the blue.

The Mariner

"Wreck and stray and castaway."

—Swinburne

Once more adrift.
O'er dappling sea and broad lagoon,
O'er frowning cliff and yellow dune,
The long, warm lights of afternoon
    Like jewel dustings sift.

Once more awake.
I dreamed an hour of port and quay,
Of anchorage not meant for me;
The sea, the sea, the hungry sea
    Came rolling up the break.

Once more afloat.
The billows on my moorings press't,
They drove me from my moment's rest,
And now a portless sea I breast,
    And shelterless my boat.

Once more away.
The harbour lights are growing dim,
The shore is but a purple rim,
The sea outstretches grey and grim.
    Away, away, away!

Once more at sea,
The old, old sea I used to sail,
The battling tide, the blowing gale,
The waves with ceaseless under-wail
    The life that used to be.

Lullaby of the Iroquois

Little brown baby-bird, lapped in your nest,
Wrapped in your nest,
Strapped in your nest,
Your straight little cradle-board rocks you to rest;
Its hands are your nest;
Its bands are your nest;
It swings from the down-bending branch of the oak;
You watch the camp flame, and the curling grey smoke;
But, oh, for your pretty black eyes sleep is best,—
Little brown baby of mine, go to rest.

Little brown baby-bird swinging to sleep,
Winging to sleep,
Singing to sleep,
Your wonder-black eyes that so wide open keep,
Shielding their sleep,
Unyielding to sleep,
The heron is homing, the plover is still,
The night-owl calls from his haunt on the hill,
Afar the fox barks, afar the stars peep,—
Little brown baby of mine, go to sleep.

The Corn Husker

Hard by the Indian lodges, where the bush
    Breaks in a clearing, through ill-fashioned fields,
She comes to labour, when the first still hush
    Of autumn follows large and recent yields.

Age in her fingers, hunger in her face,
    Her shoulders stooped with weight of work and years,
But rich in tawny colouring of her race,
    She comes a-field to strip the purple ears.

And all her thoughts are with the days gone by,
    Ere might's injustice banished from their lands
Her people, that to-day unheeded lie,
    Like the dead husks that rustle through her hands.

PRAIRIE GREYHOUNDS

C.P.R. "No. 1," Westbound

I swing to the sunset land—
The world of prairie, the world of plain,
The world of promise and hope and gain,
The world of gold, and the world of grain,
    And the world of the willing hand.

I carry the brave and bold—
The one who works for the nation's bread,
The one whose past is a thing that's dead,
The one who battles and beats ahead,
    And the one who goes for gold.

I swing to the "Land to Be,"
I am the power that laid its floors,
I am the guide to its western stores,
I am the key to its golden doors,
    That open alone to me.

C.P.R. "No. 2," Eastbound

I swing to the land of morn;
The grey old east with its grey old seas,
The land of leisure, the land of ease,
The land of flowers and fruits and trees,
    And the place where we were born.

Freighted with wealth I come;
For he who many a moon has spent
Far out west on adventure bent,
With well-worn pick and a folded tent,
    Is bringing his bullion home.

I never will be renowned,
As my twin that swings to the western marts,
For I am she of the humbler parts,
But I am the joy of the waiting hearts;
    For I am the Homeward-bound.

Golden—Of the Selkirks

A trail upwinds from Golden;
It leads to a land God only knows,
To the land of eternal frozen snows,
That trail unknown and olden.

And they tell a tale that is strange and wild—
Of a lovely and lonely mountain child
That went up the trail from Golden.

A child in the sweet of her womanhood,
Beautiful, tender, grave and good
As the saints in time long olden.

And the days count not, nor the weeks avail;
For the child that went up the mountain trail
Came never again to Golden.

And the watchers wept in the midnight gloom,
Where the canyons yawn and the Selkirks loom,
For the love that they knew of olden.

And April dawned, with its suns aflame,
And the eagles wheeled and the vultures came
And poised o'er the town of Golden.

God of the white eternal peaks,
Guard the dead while the vulture seeks!—
God of the days so olden.

For only God in His greatness knows
Where the mountain holly above her grows,
On the trail that leads from Golden.

THE SONGSTER

Music, music with throb and swing,
    Of a plaintive note, and long;
'Tis a note no human throat could sing,
No harp with its dulcet golden string,—
Nor lute, nor lyre with liquid ring,
    Is sweet as the robin's song.

He sings for love of the season
    When the days grow warm and long,
For the beautiful God-sent reason
    That his breast was born for song.

Calling, calling so fresh and clear,
    Through the song-sweet days of May;
Warbling there, and whistling here,
He swells his voice on the drinking ear,
On the great, wide, pulsing atmosphere
    Till his music drowns the day.

He sings for love of the season
    When the days grow warm and long,
For the beautiful God-sent reason
    That his breast was born for song.

Thistle-Down

Beyond a ridge of pine with russet tips
The west lifts to the sun her longing lips,

Her blushes stain with gold and garnet dye
The shore, the river and the wide far sky;

Like floods of wine the waters filter through
The reeds that brush our indolent canoe.

I beach the bow where sands in shadows lie;
You hold my hand a space, then speak good-bye.

Upwinds your pathway through the yellow plumes
Of goldenrod, profuse in August blooms,

And o'er its tossing sprays you toss a kiss;
A moment more, and I see only this—

The idle paddle you so lately held,
The empty bow your pliant wrist propelled,

Some thistles purpling into violet,
Their blossoms with a thousand thorns afret,

And like a cobweb, shadowy and grey,
Far floats their down—far drifts my dream away.

The Riders of the Plains[1]

Who is it lacks the knowledge? Who are the curs that dare
To whine and sneer that they do not fear the whelps in the Lion's lair?
But we of the North will answer, while life in the North remains,
Let the curs beware lest the whelps they dare are the Riders of the
    Plains;
For these are the kind whose muscle makes the power of the Lion's
    jaw,
And they keep the peace of our people and the honour of British law.

A woman has painted a picture,—'tis a neat little bit of art
The critics aver, and it roused up for her the love of the big British
    heart.
'Tis a sketch of an English bulldog that tigers would scarce attack,
And round and about and beneath him is painted the Union Jack.
With its blaze of colour, and courage, its daring in every fold,
And underneath is the title, "What we have we'll hold."
'Tis a picture plain as a mirror, but the reflex it contains
Is the counterpart of the life and heart of the Riders of the Plains;
For like to that flag and that motto, and the power of that bulldog's
    jaw,
They keep the peace of our people and the honour of British law.

These are the fearless fighters, whose life in the open lies,
Who never fail on the prairie trail 'neath the Territorial skies,
Who have laughed in the face of the bullets and the edge of the rebels'
    steel,
Who have set their ban on the lawless man with his crime beneath
    their heel;
These are the men who battle the blizzards, the suns, the rains,

---

1. The above is the Territorial pet name for the North-West Mounted Police, and is in general usage throughout Assiniboia, Saskatchewan and Alberta. At a dinner party in Boston the writer was asked, "Who are the North-West Mounted Police?" and when told that they were the pride of Canada's fighting men the questioner sneered and replied, "Ah! then they are only some of British Lion's whelps. We are not afraid of them." His companions applauded the remark.

         E. PAULINE JOHNSON

These are the famed that the North has named the "Riders of the
    Plains,"
And theirs is the might and the meaning and the strength of the
    bulldog's jaw,
While they keep the peace of the people and the honour of British law.

These are the men of action, who need not the world's renown,
For their valour is known to England's throne as a gem in the British
    crown;
These are the men who face the front, whose courage the world may
    scan,
The men who are feared by the felon, but are loved by the honest man;
These are the marrow, the pith, the cream, the best that the blood
    contains,
Who have cast their days in the valiant ways of the Riders of the
    Plains;
And theirs is the kind whose muscle makes the power of old
    England's jaw,
And they keep the peace of her people and the honour of British law.

Then down with the cur that questions,—let him slink to his craven
    den,—
For he daren't deny our hot reply as to "who are our mounted men."
He shall honour them east and westward, he shall honour them south
    and north,
He shall bare his head to that coat of red wherever that red rides forth.
'Tis well that he knows the fibre that the great North-West contains,
The North-West pride in her men that ride on the Territorial plains,—
For of such as these are the muscles and the teeth in the Lion's jaw,
And they keep the peace of our people and the honour of British law.

SILHOUETTE

The sky-line melts from russet into blue,
Unbroken the horizon, saving where
A wreath of smoke curls up the far, thin air,
And points the distant lodges of the Sioux.

Etched where the lands and cloudlands touch and die
A solitary Indian tepee stands,
The only habitation of these lands,
That roll their magnitude from sky to sky.

The tent poles lift and loom in thin relief,
The upward floating smoke ascends between,
And near the open doorway, gaunt and lean,
And shadow-like, there stands an Indian Chief.

With eyes that lost their lustre long ago,
With visage fixed and stern as fate's decree,
He looks towards the empty west, to see
The never-coming herd of buffalo.

Only the bones that bleach upon the plains,
Only the fleshless skeletons that lie
In ghastly nakedness and silence, cry
Out mutely that naught else to him remains.

A Prodigal

My heart forgot its God for love of you,
    And you forgot me, other loves to learn;
Now through a wilderness of thorn and rue
    Back to my God I turn.

And just because my God forgets the past,
    And in forgetting does not ask to know
Why I once left His arms for yours, at last
    Back to my God I go.

"Through Time and Bitter Distance"[1]

Unknown to you, I walk the cheerless shore.
    The cutting blast, the hurl of biting brine
May freeze, and still, and bind the waves at war,
    Ere you will ever know, O! Heart of mine,
That I have sought, reflected in the blue
    Of these sea depths, some shadow of your eyes;
Have hoped the laughing waves would sing of you,
    But this is all my starving sight descries—

I

Far out at sea a sail
    Bends to the freshening breeze,
Yields to the rising gale
    That sweeps the seas;

II

Yields, as a bird wind-tossed,
    To saltish waves that fling
Their spray, whose rime and frost
    Like crystals cling

III

To canvas, mast and spar,
    Till, gleaming like a gem,
She sinks beyond the far
    Horizon's hem.

---

1. For this title the author is indebted to Mr. Charles G. D. Roberts. It occurs in his sonnet, "Rain."

IV

Lost to my longing sight,
    And nothing left to me
Save an oncoming night,—
    An empty sea.

At Half-Mast

You didn't know Billy, did you? Well, Bill was one of the boys,
The greatest fellow you ever seen to racket an' raise a noise,—
An' sing! say, you never heard singing 'nless you heard Billy sing.
I used to say to him, "Billy, that voice that you've got there'd bring
A mighty sight more bank-notes to tuck away in your vest,
If only you'd go on the concert stage instead of a-ranchin' West."
An' Billy he'd jist go laughin', and say as I didn't know
A robin's whistle in springtime from a barnyard rooster's crow.
But Billy could sing, an' I sometimes think that voice lives anyhow,—
That perhaps Bill helps with the music in the place he's gone to now.

The last time that I seen him was the day he rode away;
He was goin' acrost the plain to catch the train for the East next day.
'Twas the only time I ever seen poor Bill that he didn't laugh
Or sing, an' kick up a rumpus an' racket around, and chaff,
For he'd got a letter from his folks that said for to hurry home,
For his mother was dyin' away down East an' she wanted Bill to come.
Say, but the feller took it hard, but he saddled up right away,
An' started across the plains to take the train for the East, next day.
Sometimes I lie awake a-nights jist a-thinkin' of the rest,
For that was the great big blizzard day, when the wind come down
    from west,
An' the snow piled up like mountains an' we couldn't put foot outside,
But jist set into the shack an' talked of Bill on his lonely ride.
We talked of the laugh he threw us as he went at the break o' day,
An' we talked of the poor old woman dyin' a thousand mile away.

Well, Dan O'Connell an' I went out to search at the end of the week,
Fer all of us fellers thought a lot,—a lot that we darsn't speak.
We'd been up the trail about forty mile, an' was talkin' of turnin' back,
But Dan, well, he wouldn't give in, so we kep' right on to the railroad
    track.
As soon as we sighted them telegraph wires says Dan, "Say, bless my
    soul!
Ain't that there Bill's red handkerchief tied half way up that pole?"
Yes, sir, there she was, with her ends a-flippin' an' flyin' in the wind,

An' underneath was the envelope of Bill's letter tightly pinned.
"Why, he must a-boarded the train right here," says Dan, but I kinder
    knew
That underneath them snowdrifts we would find a thing or two;
Fer he'd writ on that there paper, "Been lost fer hours,—all hope is
    past.
You'll find me, boys, where my handkerchief is flyin' at half-mast."

The Sleeping Giant

(Thunder Bay, Lake Superior)

When did you sink to your dreamless sleep
    Out there in your thunder bed?
Where the tempests sweep,
And the waters leap,
    And the storms rage overhead.

Were you lying there on your couch alone
    Ere Egypt and Rome were born?
Ere the Age of Stone,
Or the world had known
    The Man with the Crown of Thorn.

The winds screech down from the open west,
    And the thunders beat and break
On the amethyst
Of your rugged breast,—
    But you never arise or wake.

You have locked your past, and you keep the key
    In your heart 'neath the westing sun,
Where the mighty sea
And its shores will be
    Storm-swept till the world is done.

THE QUILL WORKER

Plains, plains, and the prairie land which the sunlight floods and fills,
To the north the open country, southward the Cyprus Hills;
Never a bit of woodland, never a rill that flows,
Only a stretch of cactus beds, and the wild, sweet prairie rose;
Never a habitation, save where in the far south-west
A solitary tepee lifts its solitary crest,
Where Neykia in the doorway, crouched in the red sunshine,
Broiders her buckskin mantle with the quills of the porcupine.

Neykia, the Sioux chief's daughter, she with the foot that flies,
She with the hair of midnight and the wondrous midnight eyes,
She with the deft brown fingers, she with the soft, slow smile,
She with the voice of velvet and the thoughts that dream the while,—
"Whence come the vague to-morrows? Where do the yesters fly?
What is beyond the border of the prairie and the sky?
Does the maid in the Land of Morning sit in the red sunshine,
Broidering her buckskin mantle with the quills of the porcupine?"

So Neykia, in the westland, wonders and works away,
Far from the fret and folly of the "Land of Waking Day."
And many the pale-faced trader who stops at the tepee door
For a smile from the sweet, shy worker, and a sigh when the hour is
    o'er.
For they know of a young red hunter who oftentimes has stayed
To rest and smoke with her father, tho' his eyes were on the maid;
And the moons will not be many ere she in the red sunshine
Will broider his buckskin mantle with the quills of the porcupine.

Guard of the Eastern Gate

Halifax sits on her hills by the sea
    In the might of her pride,—
Invincible, terrible, beautiful, she
    With a sword at her side.

To right and to left of her, battlements rear
    And fortresses frown;
While she sits on her throne without favour or fear
    With her cannon as crown.

Coast guard and sentinel, watch of the weal
    Of a nation she keeps;
But her hand is encased in a gauntlet of steel,
    And her thunder but sleeps.

At Crow's Nest Pass

At Crow's Nest Pass the mountains rend
Themselves apart, the rivers wend
    A lawless course about their feet,
    And breaking into torrents beat
In useless fury where they blend
        At Crow's Nest Pass.

The nesting eagle, wise, discreet,
Wings up the gorge's lone retreat
And makes some barren crag her friend
        At Crow's Nest Pass.

Uncertain clouds, half-high, suspend
Their shifting vapours, and contend
    With rocks that suffer not defeat;
    And snows, and suns, and mad winds meet
To battle where the cliffs defend
        At Crow's Nest Pass.

"Give Us Barabbas"[1]

There was a man—a Jew of kingly blood,
    But of the people—poor and lowly born,
Accused of blasphemy of God, He stood
    Before the Roman Pilate, while in scorn
The multitude demanded it was fit
    That one should suffer for the people, while
Another be released, absolved, acquit,
    To live his life out virtuous or vile.

"Whom will ye have—Barabbas or this Jew?"
Pilate made answer to the mob, "The choice
Is yours; I wash my hands of this, and you,
    Do as you will." With one vast ribald voice
The populace arose and, shrieking, cried,
    "Give us Barabbas, we condone his deeds!"
And He of Nazareth was crucified—
    Misjudged, condemned, dishonoured for their needs.

And down these nineteen centuries anew
    Comes the hoarse-throated, brutalized refrain,
"Give us Barabbas, crucify the Jew!"
    Once more a man must bear a nation's stain,—
And that in France, the chivalrous, whose lore
    Made her the flower of knightly age gone by.
Now she lies hideous with a leprous sore
    No skill can cure—no pardon purify.

And an indignant world, transfixed with hate
    Of such disease, cries, as in Herod's time,
Pointing its finger at her festering state,
    "Room for the leper, and her leprous crime!"
And France, writhing from years of torment, cries
    Out in her anguish, "Let this Jew endure,

---

1. Written after Dreyfus was exiled.

Damned and disgraced, vicarious sacrifice.
  The honour of my army is secure."

And, vampire-like, that army sucks the blood
  From out a martyr's veins, and strips his crown
Of honour from him, and his herohood
  Flings in the dust, and cuts his manhood down.
Hide from your God, O! ye that did this act!
  With lesser crimes the halls of Hell are paved.
Your army's honour may be still intact,
  Unstained, unsoiled, unspotted,—but unsaved.

YOUR MIRROR FRAME

Methinks I see your mirror frame,
    Ornate with photographs of them.
Place mine therein, for, all the same,
    I'll have my little laughs at them.

For girls may come, and girls may go,
    I think I have the best of them;
And yet this photograph I know
    You'll toss among the rest of them.

I cannot even hope that you
    Will put me in your locket, dear;
Nor costly frame will I look through,
    Nor bide in your breast pocket, dear.

For none your heart monopolize,
    You favour such a nest of them.
So I but hope your roving eyes
    Seek mine among the rest of them.

For saucy sprite, and noble dame,
    And many a dainty maid of them
Will greet me in your mirror frame,
    And share your kisses laid on them.

And yet, sometimes I fancy, dear,
    You hold me as the best of them.
So I'm content if I appear
    To-night with all the rest of them.

The City and the Sea

I

To none the city bends a servile knee;
　　Purse-proud and scornful, on her heights she stands,
And at her feet the great white moaning sea
　　Shoulders incessantly the grey-gold sands,—
One the Almighty's child since time began,
　　And one the might of Mammon, born of clods;
For all the city is the work of man,
　　But all the sea is God's.

II

And she—between the ocean and the town—
　　Lies cursed of one and by the other blest:
Her staring eyes, her long drenched hair, her gown,
　　Sea-laved and soiled and dank above her breast.
She, image of her God since life began,
　　She, but the child of Mammon, born of clods,
Her broken body spoiled and spurned of man,
　　But her sweet soul is God's.

FIRE-FLOWERS

And only where the forest fires have sped,
    Scorching relentlessly the cool north lands,
A sweet wild flower lifts its purple head,
And, like some gentle spirit sorrow-fed,
    It hides the scars with almost human hands.

And only to the heart that knows of grief,
    Of desolating fire, of human pain,
There comes some purifying sweet belief,
Some fellow-feeling beautiful, if brief.
    And life revives, and blossoms once again.

A Toast

There's wine in the cup, Vancouver,
    And there's warmth in my heart for you,
While I drink to your health, your youth, and your wealth,
    And the things that you yet will do.
In a vintage rare and olden,
    With a flavour fine and keen,
Fill the glass to the edge, while I stand up to pledge
    My faith to my western queen.

Then here's a Ho! Vancouver, in wine of the bonniest hue,
    With a hand on my hip and the cup at my lip,
And a love in my life for you.
    For you are a jolly good fellow, with a great, big heart, I know;
So I drink this toast
To the "Queen of the Coast."
    Vancouver, here's a Ho!

And here's to the days that are coming,
    And here's to the days that are gone,
And here's to your gold and your spirit bold,
    And your luck that has held its own;
And here's to your hands so sturdy,
    And here's to your hearts so true,
And here's to the speed of the day decreed
    That brings me again to you.

Then here's a Ho! Vancouver, in wine of the bonniest hue,
    With a hand on my hip and the cup at my lip,
And a love in my life for you.
    For you are a jolly good fellow, with a great, big heart, I know;
So I drink this toast
To the "Queen of the Coast."
    Vancouver, here's a Ho!

Lady Icicle

Little Lady Icicle is dreaming in the north-land
And gleaming in the north-land, her pillow all a-glow;
 For the frost has come and found her
 With an ermine robe around her
Where little Lady Icicle lies dreaming in the snow.

Little Lady Icicle is waking in the north-land,
And shaking in the north-land her pillow to and fro;
 And the hurricane a-skirling
 Sends the feathers all a-whirling
Where little Lady Icicle is waking in the snow.

Little Lady Icicle is laughing in the north-land,
And quaffing in the north-land her wines that overflow;
 All the lakes and rivers crusting
 That her finger-tips are dusting,
Where little Lady Icicle is laughing in the snow.

Little Lady Icicle is singing in the north-land,
And bringing from the north-land a music wild and low;
 And the fairies watch and listen
 Where her silver slippers glisten,
As little Lady Icicle goes singing through the snow.

Little Lady Icicle is coming from the north-land,
Benumbing all the north-land where'er her feet may go;
 With a fringe of frost before her
 And a crystal garment o'er her,
Little Lady Icicle is coming with the snow.

The Legend of Qu'Appelle Valley

I am the one who loved her as my life,
    Had watched her grow to sweet young womanhood;
Won the dear privilege to call her wife,
    And found the world, because of her, was good.
I am the one who heard the spirit voice,
    Of which the paleface settlers love to tell;
From whose strange story they have made their choice
    Of naming this fair valley the "Qu'Appelle."

She had said fondly in my eager ear—
    "When Indian summer smiles with dusky lip,
Come to the lakes, I will be first to hear
    The welcome music of thy paddle dip.
I will be first to lay in thine my hand,
    To whisper words of greeting on the shore;
And when thou would'st return to thine own land,
    I'll go with thee, thy wife for evermore."

Not yet a leaf had fallen, not a tone
    Of frost upon the plain ere I set forth,
Impatient to possess her as my own—
    This queen of all the women of the North.
I rested not at even or at dawn,
    But journeyed all the dark and daylight through—
Until I reached the Lakes, and, hurrying on,
    I launched upon their bosom my canoe.

Of sleep or hunger then I took no heed,
    But hastened o'er their leagues of waterways;
But my hot heart outstripped my paddle's speed
    And waited not for distance or for days,
But flew before me swifter than the blade
    Of magic paddle ever cleaved the Lake,
Eager to lay its love before the maid,
    And watch the lovelight in her eyes awake.

So the long days went slowly drifting past;
　　It seemed that half my life must intervene
Before the morrow, when I said at last—
　　"One more day's journey and I win my queen!"
I rested then, and, drifting, dreamed the more
　　Of all the happiness I was to claim,—
When suddenly from out the shadowed shore,
　　I heard a voice speak tenderly my name.

"Who calls?" I answered; no reply; and long
　　I stilled my paddle blade and listened. Then
Above the night wind's melancholy song
　　I heard distinctly that strange voice again—
A woman's voice, that through the twilight came
　　Like to a soul unborn—a song unsung.

I leaned and listened—yes, she spoke my name,
　　And then I answered in the quaint French tongue,
"Qu'Appelle? Qu'Appelle?" No answer, and the night
　　Seemed stiller for the sound, till round me fell
The far-off echoes from the far-off height—
　　"Qu'Appelle?" my voice came back, "Qu'Appelle? Qu'Appelle?"
This—and no more; I called aloud until
　　I shuddered as the gloom of night increased,
And, like a pallid spectre wan and chill,
　　The moon arose in silence in the east.

I dare not linger on the moment when
　　My boat I beached beside her tepee door;
I heard the wail of women and of men,—
　　I saw the death-fires lighted on the shore.
No language tells the torture or the pain,
　　The bitterness that flooded all my life,—
When I was led to look on her again,
　　That queen of women pledged to be my wife.
To look upon the beauty of her face,
　　The still closed eyes, the lips that knew no breath;
To look, to learn,—to realize my place
　　Had been usurped by my one rival—Death.

　　　　　　　　　　　　　　　E. PAULINE JOHNSON

A storm of wrecking sorrow beat and broke
    About my heart, and life shut out its light
Till through my anguish some one gently spoke,
    And said, "Twice did she call for thee last night."

I started up—and bending o'er my dead,
    Asked when did her sweet lips in silence close.
"She called thy name—then passed away," they said,
    "Just on the hour whereat the moon arose."

Among the lonely Lakes I go no more,
    For she who made their beauty is not there;
The paleface rears his tepee on the shore
    And says the vale is fairest of the fair.
Full many years have vanished since, but still
    The voyageurs beside the campfire tell
How, when the moonrise tips the distant hill,
    They hear strange voices through the silence swell.
The paleface loves the haunted lakes they say,
    And journeys far to watch their beauty spread
Before his vision; but to me the day,
    The night, the hour, the seasons are all dead.
I listen heartsick, while the hunters tell
    Why white men named the valley The Qu'Appelle.

THE ART OF ALMA-TADEMA

There is no song his colours cannot sing,
    For all his art breathes melody, and tunes
The fine, keen beauty that his brushes bring
    To murmuring marbles and to golden Junes.

The music of those marbles you can hear
    In every crevice, where the deep green stains
Have sunken when the grey days of the year
    Spilled leisurely their warm, incessant rains

That, lingering, forget to leave the ledge,
    But drenched into the seams, amid the hush
Of ages, leaving but the silent pledge
    To waken to the wonder of his brush.

And at the Master's touch the marbles leap
    To life, the creamy onyx and the skins
Of copper-coloured leopards, and the deep,
    Cool basins where the whispering water wins

Reflections from the gold and glowing sun,
    And tints from warm, sweet human flesh, for fair
And subtly lithe and beautiful, leans one—
    A goddess with a wealth of tawny hair.

E. PAULINE JOHNSON

Good-Bye

Sounds of the seas grow fainter,
    Sounds of the sands have sped;
The sweep of gales,
The far white sails,
    Are silent, spent and dead.

Sounds of the days of summer
    Murmur and die away,
And distance hides
The long, low tides,
    As night shuts out the day.

MISCELLANEOUS POEMS

(These miscellaneous poems are all of later date.)

IN GREY DAYS

Measures of oil for others,
 Oil and red wine,
Lips laugh and drink, but never
 Are the lips mine.

Worlds at the feet of others,
 Power gods have known,
Hearts for the favoured round me
 Mine beats, alone.

Fame offering to others
 Chaplets of bays,
I with no crown of laurels,
 Only grey days.

Sweet human love for others,
 Deep as the sea,
God-sent unto my neighbour—
 But not to me.

Sometime I'll wrest from others
 More than all this,
I shall demand from Heaven
 Far sweeter bliss.

What profit then to others,
 Laughter and wine?
I'll have what most they covet—
 Death, will be mine.

BRANDON

(Acrostic)

Born on the breast of the prairie, she smiles to her sire—the sun,
Robed in the wealth of her wheat-lands, gift of her mothering soil,
Affluence knocks at her gateways, opulence waits to be won.
Nuggets of gold are her acres, yielding and yellow with spoil,
Dream of the hungry millions, dawn of the food-filled age,
Over the starving tale of want her fingers have turned the page;
Nations will nurse at her storehouse, and God gives her grain for wage.

The Indian Corn Planter

He needs must leave the trapping and the chase,
    For mating game his arrows ne'er despoil,
And from the hunter's heaven turn his face,
    To wring some promise from the dormant soil.

He needs must leave the lodge that wintered him,
    The enervating fires, the blanket bed—
The women's dulcet voices, for the grim
    Realities of labouring for bread.

So goes he forth beneath the planter's moon
    With sack of seed that pledges large increase,
His simple pagan faith knows night and noon,
    Heat, cold, seedtime and harvest shall not cease.

And yielding to his needs, this honest sod,
    Brown as the hand that tills it, moist with rain,
Teeming with ripe fulfilment, true as God,
    With fostering richness, mothers every grain.

The Cattle Country

Up the dusk-enfolded prairie,
    Foot-falls, soft and sly,
Velvet cushioned, wild and wary,
    Then—the coyote's cry.

Rush of hoofs, and roar and rattle,
    Beasts of blood and breed,
Twenty thousand frightened cattle,
    Then—the wild stampede.

Pliant lasso circling wider
    In the frenzied flight—
Loping horse and cursing rider,
    Plunging through the night.

Rim of dawn the darkness losing
    Trail of blackened soil;
Perfume of the sage brush oozing
    On the air like oil.

Foothills to the Rockies lifting
    Brown, and blue, and green,
Warm Alberta sunlight drifting
    Over leagues between.

That's the country of the ranges,
Plain and prairie land,
And the God who never changes
    Holds it in His hand.

E. PAULINE JOHNSON

Autumn's Orchestra

(Inscribed to One Beyond Seas)

Know by the thread of music woven through
This fragile web of cadences I spin,
That I have only caught these songs since you
Voiced them upon your haunting violin.

The Overture

October's orchestra plays softly on
The northern forest with its thousand strings,
And Autumn, the conductor wields anon
The Golden-rod—The baton that he swings.

The Firs

There is a lonely minor chord that sings
Faintly and far along the forest ways,
When the firs finger faintly on the strings
Of that rare violin the night wind plays,
Just as it whispered once to you and me
Beneath the English pines beyond the sea.

Mosses

The lost wind wandering, forever grieves
    Low overhead,
Above grey mosses whispering of leaves
    Fallen and dead.
And through the lonely night sweeps their refrain
Like Chopin's prelude, sobbing 'neath the rain.

The Vine

The wild grape mantling the trail and tree,
Festoons in graceful veils its drapery,
Its tendrils cling, as clings the memory stirred
By some evasive haunting tune, twice heard.

The Maple

I

It is the blood-hued maple straight and strong,
Voicing abroad its patriotic song.

II

Its daring colours bravely flinging forth
The ensign of the Nation of the North.

Hare-Bell

Elfin bell in azure dress,
Chiming all day long,
Ringing through the wilderness
Dulcet notes of song.
Daintiest of forest flowers
Weaving like a spell—
Music through the Autumn hours,
Little Elfin bell.

The Giant Oak

And then the sound of marching armies 'woke
Amid the branches of the soldier oak,
And tempests ceased their warring cry, and dumb
The lashing storms that muttered, overcome,
Choked by the heralding of battle smoke,
When these gnarled branches beat their martial drum.

Aspens

A sweet high treble threads its silvery song,
Voice of the restless aspen, fine and thin
It trills its pure soprano, light and long—
Like the vibretto of a mandolin.

Finale

The cedar trees have sung their vesper hymn,
And now the music sleeps—
Its benediction falling where the dim
Dusk of the forest creeps.
Mute grows the great concerto—and the light
Of day is darkening, Good-night, Good-night.
But through the night time I shall hear within
The murmur of these trees,
The calling of your distant violin
Sobbing across the seas,
And waking wind, and star-reflected light
Shall voice my answering. Good-night, Good-night.

The Trail to Lillooet

Sob of fall, and song of forest, come you here on haunting quest,
Calling through the seas and silence, from God's country of the west.
Where the mountain pass is narrow, and the torrent white and strong,
Down its rocky-throated canyon, sings its golden-throated song.

You are singing there together through the God-begotten nights,
And the leaning stars are listening above the distant heights
That lift like points of opal in the crescent coronet
About whose golden setting sweeps the trail to Lillooet.

Trail that winds and trail that wanders, like a cobweb hanging high,
Just a hazy thread outlining mid-way of the stream and sky,
Where the Fraser River canyon yawns its pathway to the sea,
But half the world has shouldered up between its song and me.

Here, the placid English August, and the sea-encircled miles,
There—God's copper-coloured sunshine beating through the lonely
    aisles
Where the waterfalls and forest voice for ever their duet,
And call across the canyon on the trail to Lillooet.

Canada

(Acrostic)

Crown of her, young Vancouver; crest of her, old Quebec;
Atlantic and far Pacific sweeping her, keel to deck.
North of her, ice and arctics; southward a rival's stealth;
Aloft, her Empire's pennant; below, her nation's wealth.
Daughter of men and markets, bearing within her hold,
Appraised at highest value, cargoes of grain and gold.

The Lifting of the Mist

All the long day the vapours played
    At blindfold in the city streets,
Their elfin fingers caught and stayed
    The sunbeams, as they wound their sheets
Into a filmy barricade
    'Twixt earth and where the sunlight beats.

A vagrant band of mischiefs these,
    With wings of grey and cobweb gown;
They live along the edge of seas,
    And creeping out on foot of down,
They chase and frolic, frisk and tease
    At blind-man's buff with all the town.

And when at eventide the sun
    Breaks with a glory through their grey,
The vapour-fairies, one by one,
Outspread their wings and float away
In clouds of colouring, that run
    Wine-like along the rim of day.

Athwart the beauty and the breast
    Of purpling airs they twirl and twist,
Then float away to some far rest,
    Leaving the skies all colour-kiss't—
A glorious and a golden West
    That greets the Lifting of the Mist.

The Homing Bee

You are belted with gold, little brother of mine,
    Yellow gold, like the sun
That spills in the west, as a chalice of wine
    When feasting is done.

You are gossamer-winged, little brother of mine,
    Tissue winged, like the mist
That broods where the marshes melt into a line
    Of vapour sun-kissed.

You are laden with sweets, little brother of mine,
    Flower sweets, like the touch
Of hands we have longed for, of arms that entwine,
    Of lips that love much.

You are better than I, little brother of mine,
    Than I, human-souled,
For you bring from the blossoms and red summer shine,
    For others, your gold.

The Lost Lagoon

It is dusk on the Lost Lagoon,
And we two dreaming the dusk away,
Beneath the drift of a twilight grey,
Beneath the drowse of an ending day,
And the curve of a golden moon.

It is dark in the Lost Lagoon,
And gone are the depths of haunting blue,
The grouping gulls, and the old canoe,
The singing firs, and the dusk and—you,
And gone is the golden moon.

O! lure of the Lost Lagoon,—
I dream to-night that my paddle blurs
The purple shade where the seaweed stirs,
I hear the call of the singing firs
In the hush of the golden moon.

THE TRAIN DOGS

Out of the night and the north;
    Savage of breed and of bone,
Shaggy and swift comes the yelping band,
Freighters of fur from the voiceless land
    That sleeps in the Arctic zone.

Laden with skins from the north,
    Beaver and bear and raccoon,
Marten and mink from the polar belts,
Otter and ermine and sable pelts—
    The spoils of the hunter's moon.

Out of the night and the north,
    Sinewy, fearless and fleet,
Urging the pack through the pathless snow,
The Indian driver, calling low,
    Follows with moccasined feet.

Ships of the night and the north,
    Freighters on prairies and plains,
Carrying cargoes from field and flood
They scent the trail through their wild red blood,
    The wolfish blood in their veins.

THE KING'S CONSORT

I

Love, was it yesternoon, or years agone,
    You took in yours my hands,
And placed me close beside you on the throne
    Of Oriental lands?

The truant hour came back at dawn to-day,
    Across the hemispheres,
And bade my sleeping soul retrace its way
    These many hundred years.

And all my wild young life returned, and ceased
    The years that lie between,
When you were King of Egypt, and The East,
    And I was Egypt's queen.

II

I feel again the lengths of silken gossamer enfold
My body and my limbs in robes of emerald and gold.
I feel the heavy sunshine, and the weight of languid heat
That crowned the day you laid the royal jewels at my feet.

You wound my throat with jacinths, green and glist'ning serpent-wise,
My hot, dark throat that pulsed beneath the ardour of your eyes;
And centuries have failed to cool the memory of your hands
That bound about my arms those massive, pliant golden bands.

You wreathed around my wrists long ropes of coral and of jade,
And beaten gold that clung like coils of kisses love-inlaid;
About my naked ankles tawny topaz chains you wound,
With clasps of carven onyx, ruby-rimmed and golden bound.

But not for me the Royal Pearls to bind about my hair,
"Pearls were too passionless," you said, for one like me to wear,

I must have all the splendour, all the jewels warm as wine,
But pearls so pale and cold were meant for other flesh than mine.

But all the blood-warm beauty of the gems you thought my due
Were pallid as a pearl beside the love I gave to you;
O! Love of mine come back across the years that lie between,
When you were King of Egypt—Dear, and I was Egypt's Queen.

When George Was King

Cards, and swords, and a lady's love,
That is a tale worth reading,
An insult veiled, a downcast glove,
And rapiers leap unheeding.
 And 'tis O! for the brawl,
 The thrust, the fall,
And the foe at your feet a-bleeding.

Tales of revel at wayside inns,
The goblets gaily filling,
Braggarts boasting a thousand sins,
Though none can boast a shilling.
 And 'tis O! for the wine,
 The frothing stein,
And the clamour of cups a-spilling.

Tales of maidens in rich brocade,
Powder and puff and patches,
Gallants lilting a serenade
Of old-time trolls and catches.
 And 'tis O! for the lips
 And the finger tips,
And the kiss that the boldest snatches.

Tales of buckle and big rosette,
The slender shoe adorning,
Of curtseying through the minuet
With laughter, love, or scorning.
 And 'tis O! for the shout
 Of the roustabout,
As he hies him home in the morning.

Cards and swords, and a lady's love,
Give to the tale God-speeding,
War and wassail, and perfumed glove,
And all that's rare in reading.

And 'tis O! for the ways
Of the olden days,
And a life that was worth the leading.

DAY DAWN

All yesterday the thought of you was resting in my soul,
And when sleep wandered o'er the world that very thought she stole
To fill my dreams with splendour such as stars could not eclipse,
And in the morn I wakened with your name upon my lips.

Awakened, my beloved, to the morning of your eyes,
Your splendid eyes, so full of clouds, wherein a shadow tries
To overcome the flame that melts into the world of grey,
As coming suns dissolve the dark that veils the edge of day.

Cool drifts the air at dawn of day, cool lies the sleeping dew,
But all my heart is burning, for it woke from dreams of you;
And O! these longing eyes of mine look out and only see
A dying night, a waking day, and calm on all but me.

So gently creeps the morning through the heavy air,
The dawn grey-garbed and velvet-shod is wandering everywhere
To wake the slumber-laden hours that leave their dreamless rest,
With outspread, laggard wings to court the pillows of the west.

Up from the earth a moisture steals with odours fresh and soft,
A smell of moss and grasses warm with dew, and far aloft
The stars are growing colourless, while drooping in the west,
A late, wan moon is paling in a sky of amethyst.

The passing of the shadows, as they waft their pinions near,
Has stirred a tender wind within the night-hushed atmosphere,
That in its homeless wanderings sobs in an undertone
An echo to my heart that sobbing calls for you alone.

The night is gone, beloved, and another day set free,
Another day of hunger for the one I may not see.
What care I for the perfect dawn? the blue and empty skies?
The night is always mine without the morning of your eyes.

THE ARCHERS

I

Stripped to the waist, his copper-coloured skin
Red from the smouldering heat of hate within,
Lean as a wolf in winter, fierce of mood—
As all wild things that hunt for foes, or food—
War paint adorning breast and thigh and face,
Armed with the ancient weapons of his race,
A slender ashen bow, deer sinew strung,
And flint-tipped arrow each with poisoned tongue,—
Thus does the Red man stalk to death his foe,
And sighting him strings silently his bow,
Takes his unerring aim, and straight and true
The arrow cuts in flight the forest through,
A flint which never made for mark and missed,
And finds the heart of his antagonist.
Thus has he warred and won since time began,
Thus does the Indian bring to earth his man.

II

Ungarmented, save for a web that lies
In fleecy folds across his impish eyes,
A tiny archer takes his way intent
On mischief, which is his especial bent.
Across his shoulder lies a quiver, filled
With arrows dipped in honey, thrice distilled
From all the roses brides have ever worn
Since that first wedding out of Eden born.
Beneath a cherub face and dimpled smile
This youthful hunter hides a heart of guile;
His arrows aimed at random fly in quest
Of lodging-place within some blameless breast.
But those he wounds die happily, and so

Blame not young Cupid with his dart and bow:
Thus has he warred and won since time began,
Transporting into Heaven both maid and man.

THE WOLF

Like a grey shadow lurking in the light,
He ventures forth along the edge of night;
With silent foot he scouts the coulie's rim
And scents the carrion awaiting him.
His savage eyeballs lurid with a flare
Seen but in unfed beasts which leave their lair
To wrangle with their fellows for a meal
Of bones ill-covered. Sets he forth to steal,
To search and snarl and forage hungrily;
A worthless prairie vagabond is he.
Luckless the settler's heifer which astray
Falls to his fangs and violence a prey;
Useless her blatant calling when his teeth
Are fast upon her quivering flank—beneath
His fell voracity she falls and dies
With inarticulate and piteous cries,
Unheard, unheeded in the barren waste,
To be devoured with savage greed and haste.
Up the horizon once again he prowls
And far across its desolation howls;
Sneaking and satisfied his lair he gains
And leaves her bones to bleach upon the plains.

THE MAN IN CHRYSANTHEMUM LAND

Written for "The Spectator"

There's a brave little berry-brown man
At the opposite side of the earth;
Of the White, and the Black, and the Tan,
He's the smallest in compass and girth.
O! he's little, and lively, and Tan,
And he's showing the world what he's worth.
For his nation is born, and its birth
Is for hardihood, courage, and sand,
    So you take off your cap
    To the brave little Jap
Who fights for Chrysanthemum Land.

Near the house that the little man keeps,
There's a Bug-a-boo building its lair;
It prowls, and it growls, and it sleeps
At the foot of his tiny back stair.
But the little brown man never sleeps,
For the Brownie will battle the Bear—
He has soldiers and ships to command;
    So take off you cap
    To the brave little Jap
Who fights for Chrysanthemum Land.

Uncle Sam stands a-watching near by,
With his finger aside of his nose—
John Bull with a wink in his eye,
Looks round to see how the wind blows—
O! jolly old John, with his eye
Ever set on the East and its woes.
More than hoeing their own little rows
These wary old wags understand,
    But they take off their caps
    To the brave little Japs
Who fight for Chrysanthemum Land.

Now he's given us Geishas, and themes
For operas, stories, and plays,
His silks and his chinas are dreams,
And we copy his quaint little ways;
O! we look on his land in our dreams,
But his value we failed to appraise,
For he'll gather his laurels and bays—
His Cruisers and Columns are manned,
    And we take off our caps
    To the brave little Japs
Who fight for Chrysanthemum Land.

Calgary of the Plains

Not of the seething cities with their swarming human hives,
Their fetid airs, their reeking streets, their dwarfed and poisoned lives,
Not of the buried yesterdays, but of the days to be,
The glory and the gateway of the yellow West is she.

The Northern Lights dance down her plains with soft and silvery feet,
The sunrise gilds her prairies when the dawn and daylight meet;
Along her level lands the fitful southern breezes sweep,
And beyond her western windows the sublime old mountains sleep.

The Redman haunts her portals, and the Paleface treads her streets,
The Indian's stealthy footstep with the course of commerce meets,
And hunters whisper vaguely of the half forgotten tales
Of phantom herds of bison lurking on her midnight trails.

Not hers the lore of olden lands, their laurels and their bays;
But what are these, compared to one of all her perfect days?
For naught can buy the jewel that upon her forehead lies—
The cloudless sapphire Heaven of her territorial skies.

The Ballad of Yaada[1]

(A Legend of the Pacific Coast)

There are fires on Lulu Island, and the sky is opalescent
  With the pearl and purple tinting from the smouldering of peat.
And the Dream Hills lift their summits in a sweeping, hazy crescent,
  With the Capilano canyon at their feet.

There are fires on Lulu Island, and the smoke, uplifting, lingers
  In a faded scarf of fragrance as it creeps across the day,
And the Inlet and the Narrows blur beneath its silent fingers,
  And the canyon is enfolded in its grey.

But the sun its face is veiling like a cloistered nun at vespers;
  As towards the alter candles of the night a censer swings,
And the echo of tradition wakes from slumbering and whispers,
  Where the Capilano river sobs and sings.

It was Yaada, lovely Yaada, who first taught the stream its sighing,
  For 'twas silent till her coming, and 'twas voiceless as the shore;
But throughout the great forever it will sing the song undying
  That the lips of lovers sing for evermore.

He was chief of all the Squamish, and he ruled the coastal waters—
  And he warred upon her people in the distant Charlotte Isles;
She, a winsome basket weaver, daintiest of Haida daughters,
  Made him captive to her singing and her smiles.

Till his hands forgot to havoc and his weapons lost their lusting,
  Till his stormy eyes allured her from the land of Totem Poles,
Till she followed where he called her, followed with a woman's
    trusting,
  To the canyon where the Capilano rolls.

---

1. "The Ballad of Yaada" is the last complete poem written by the author. It was placed for publication with the "Saturday Night" of Toronto, and did not appear in print until several months after Miss Johnson's death.

And the women of the Haidas plied in vain their magic power,
	Wailed for many moons her absence, wailed for many moons their
	prayer,
"Bring her back, O Squamish foeman, bring to us our Yaada flower!"
	But the silence only answered their despair.

But the men were swift to battle, swift to cross the coastal water,
	Swift to war and swift of weapon, swift to paddle trackless miles,
Crept with stealth along the canyon, stole her from her love and
	brought her
	Once again unto the distant Charlotte Isles.

But she faded, ever faded, and her eyes were ever turning
	Southward toward the Capilano, while her voice had hushed its
	song,
And her riven heart repeated words that on her lips were burning:
	"Not to friend—but unto foeman I belong.

"Give me back my Squamish lover—though you hate, I still must love
	him.
	"Give me back the rugged canyon where my heart must ever be—
Where his lodge awaits my coming, and the Dream Hills lift above
	him,
	And the Capilano learned its song from me."

But through long-forgotten seasons, moons too many to be numbered,
	He yet waited by the canyon—she called across the years,
And the soul within the river, though centuries had slumbered,
	Woke to sob a song of womanly tears.

For her little, lonely spirit sought the Capilano canyon,
	When she died among the Haidas in the land of Totem Poles,
And you yet may hear her singing to her lover-like companion,
	If you listen to the river as it rolls.

But 'tis only when the pearl and purple smoke is idly swinging
	From the fires on Lulu Island to the hazy mountain crest,
That the undertone of sobbing echoes through the river's singing,
	In the Capilano canyon of the West.

"And He Said, Fight On"[1]

(Tennyson)

Time and its ally, Dark Disarmament,
    Have compassed me about,
Have massed their armies, and on battle bent
    My forces put to rout;
But though I fight alone, and fall, and die,
    Talk terms of Peace? Not I.

They war upon my fortress, and their guns
    Are shattering its walls;
My army plays the cowards' part, and runs,
    Pierced by a thousand balls;
They call for my surrender. I reply,
    "Give quarter now? Not I."

They've shot my flag to ribbons, but in rents
    It floats above the height;
Their ensign shall not crown my battlements
    While I can stand and fight.
I fling defiance at them as I cry,
    "Capitulate? Not I."

---

1. E. Pauline Johnson died March 7th, 1913. Shortly after the doctors told her that her illness would be her final one, she wrote the above poem, taking a line from Tennyson as her theme.

A Note About the Author

E. Pauline Johnson (1861–1913) was a Canadian poet and actress. Also known by her stage name Tekahionwake, Johnson was born to an English mother and a Mohawk father in Six Nations, Ontario. Johnson suffered from illness as a child, keeping her from school and encouraging her self-education through the works of Longfellow, Tennyson, Browning, Byron, and Keats. Despite the racism suffered by Canada's indigenous people, Johnson was encouraged to learn about her Mohawk heritage, much of which came from her paternal grandfather John Smoke Johnson, who shared with her and her siblings his knowledge of the oral tradition of their people. In the 1880s, Johnson began acting and writing for small theater productions, finding success in 1892 with a popular solo act emphasizing her duel heritage. In these performances, Johnson would wear both indigenous and Victorian English costumes, reciting original poetry for each persona. As a poet, she wrote prolifically for such periodicals as *Globe* and *Saturday Night*, publishing her first collection, *The White Wampum*, in 1895. Her death at the age of 52 prompted an outpouring of grief and celebration in Canada; at the time, Johnson's funeral was the largest in Vancouver history, attracting thousands of mourners from all walks of life.

A Note from the Publisher

Spanning many genres, from non-fiction essays to literature classics to children's books and lyric poetry, Mint Edition books showcase the master works of our time in a modern new package. The text is freshly typeset, is clean and easy to read, and features a new note about the author in each volume. Many books also include exclusive new introductory material. Every book boasts a striking new cover, which makes it as appropriate for collecting as it is for gift giving. Mint Edition books are only printed when a reader orders them, so natural resources are not wasted. We're proud that our books are never manufactured in excess and exist only in the exact quantity they need to be read and enjoyed.

bookfinity™

Discover more of your favorite classics with Bookfinity™.

- Track your reading with custom book lists.
- Get great book recommendations for your personalized Reader Type.
- Add reviews for your favorite books.
- AND MUCH MORE!

Visit **bookfinity.com** and take the fun Reader Type quiz to get started.

Enjoy our classic and modern companion pairings!